SOCr

Barcode on next page.

Barcode on next page.

D & S
VOL. 25

PART 2
DERIVATIVES

B-29
SUPERFORTRESS

in detail & scale

Alwyn T. Lloyd

2337

TAB TAB BOOKS Inc.
Blue Ridge Summit, PA 17214

 **Arms & Armour Press, Ltd.**

CONTRIBUTORS:

Dana Bell	Chuck Hansen	Peter Patterson	Air Rescue Service Historian
Carl H. Bernhardt	Gerald Hasselwander	Marilyn A. Phipps	Air Weather Service Historian
Steve Birdsall	Robert Irvin	Bill Jack Rogers	Air Force Logistics Command Historian
Peter M. Bowers	Lloyd S. Jones	Anne Rutledge	The Boeing Company Historical Services
Walter J. Boyne	Bert Kinzey	Victor D. Seely	and Public Relations Departments
George Cully	George Korade	Paul R. Schultz	Edo Corporation
R. E. Doug Fairbanks	William T. Larkins	Major Lester A. Sliter	Edwards AFB Historian
Norman Filer	Donald Little	LTC Eric Solander	National Air and Space Museum
Paul S. Friedrich	Robert Mann	Warren Thompson	Naval Weapons Center
John Fuller	Hanna Massie	Jane Trimmer	USAF Historical Research Center
Lynn Gamma	Roger A. Mead	Colonel Richard Uppstrom	USAF Museum
Harry S. Gann	David W. Menard	Vivian White	USAF Public Affairs - Books and
William Greenhalgh	James Morrison	Gordon S. Williams	Magazines Branch
LT June Green	Fred J. Olivi	Alaskan Air Command Historian	

Edited by Bert Kinzey

FIRST EDITION
FIRST PRINTING

Published in United States by

TAB BOOKS Inc.
P.O. Box 40
Blue Ridge Summit, PA 17214

Library of Congress Cataloging
in Publication Data

Lloyd, Alwyn T.
B-29 Superfortress.

(Detail & Scale series ; vol. 25)
Includes index.
1. B-29 bomber. I. Title. II. Title:
B-twenty-nine
Superfortress.
UG1242.B6L565 1986b 358.4'2 87-1471
ISBN 0-8306-8035-7 (pbk.)

First published in Great Britain in 1987
by Arms and Armour Press Limited, Link House
West Street, Poole, Dorset BH15 1LL

Distributed in Australia by
Capricorn Link (Australia) Pty. Ltd.,
P.O. Box 665
Lane Cove, New South Wales 2066,
Australia

British Library Cataloging in
Publication Data

Lloyd, Alwyn T.
B-29 Superfortress.—(Detail & Scale
series ; 25)
1. B-29 bomber—History
I. Title II. Series
623.74'63   UG1242.B6
ISBN 0-85368-839-7

Front cover: EB-29-98-BW, 45-21800, was used to carry the Bell X-1 series aircraft. A stork insignia appears on the nose of the mother ship.
(USAF)

Rear cover: TB-29-40-MO, 44-86263, was the second such airplane assigned to the 5015th Radar Evaluation Flight. All turrets were removed from this airplane. The arctic red trim was painted completely around the USAF on the wing (not around each letter). A pair of flat blade antennas were installed in the aft lower turret position. Protective boots covered the wing.
(Fox via Filer)

INTRODUCTION

This tanker cell was made up of KB-29Ps of the 91st ARefS supporting "Fox Peter Two".   (Boeing P12847)

In Volume 10 of the Detail & Scale Series, Al Lloyd covered the prototype and production versions of the B-29. From the standpoint of showing the details of the airplane itself, this was the most extensive coverage of the Superfortress ever published in a single publication. In the introduction to that book, Detail & Scale promised a second volume on the B-29, covering the derivatives to the basic airframe design. In compiling the photographs and information for this book, we have come up with the same situation that we found in covering the derivatives of the B-17. We simply cannot fit all of the derivatives into one volume, so a third volume on the B-29 will follow later in the Detail & Scale Series. It will include the B-50 and KB-50 as well as other derivatives of the B-29 design. Detail & Scale has received a large number of requests for photographic coverage of the B-50, and that is why it will be included in the B-29 Superfortress in Detail & Scale, Part 3.

This volume covers many of the unusual and varied derivatives of the B-29. The nuclear bombers, and their roles in Operation Crossroads, and Projects Silverplate and Saddletree begin the book on the following page. It was these aircraft, to include **Enola Gay** and **Bockscar,** that provided America with its first capability of nuclear deterrence. The TB-29 trainer version, RB-29/F-13 reconnaissance aircraft, SB-29 rescue versions, and WB-29 weather birds are also included. The KB-29M, YB-29J, KB-29P, and YKB-29T tankers were among the first aircraft to provide the Air Force with an in-flight refueling capability, and these are all covered in this volume.

One of the better known uses of the B-29 was that of being a "mother ship" for the early rocket planes that scorched the California skies in the late '40s and the '50s. Among these was the Bell X-1 flown by "Chuck" Yeager

when he became the first man to exceed the speed of sound. The U.S. Navy also used the B-29, designating it the P2B, as a "mother ship" for its rocket planes. The B-29 was the only aircraft to carry the XF-85 Goblin parasite fighter, and all of these uses of the B-29 to carry other aircraft are shown in this volume.

Rounding out this volume is coverage of the Tarzon bomb carriers, air resupply and communications aircraft, some unusual test aircraft, and the B-29 that now is in the Travis AFB Museum. As usual, we have included our Modeler's Section, but this time, instead of reviewing the kits, information is provided on how to build some of the derivatives that appear on these pages. Building some of these aircraft will provide the modeler with some different and unusual models not found in many collections.

Because these aircraft were not really very different from the basic B-29 design, we have not included our usual five-view drawings. Reference should be made to the five-view drawings in D&S Volume 10 for the basic B-29 airframe design. We have provided some three-view and detailed drawings to show how the basic airframe design was modified in order to develop some of these derivatives for their special and varied missions.

It is unfortunate that many aviation enthusiasts do not look past the basic design and missions for which a given aircraft was designed. In narrowing their scope of interest, they miss some of the more interesting aspects of aviation history. A close look at the derivatives on the following pages will reveal some ingenuity in airplane design, some successes and some failures, and in the case of the "mother ships," a most important part of aviation history played by derivatives of the B-29.

OPERATION CROSSROADS

Typical of the markings carried on 509th Bomb Group B-29s, other than the air attack aircraft, are shown on B-29-55-MO, 44-86401. A black circle with a 12-foot diameter was carried on the tail. An arrow was painted within the circle. None of the 509th Bomb Group bombers carried turrets. *(USAF)*

On August 6, 1945, the world's first atomic attack took place. At 2:45am Colonel Paul W. Tibbets, pilot of the **Enola Gay** of the 509th BG, departed North Field, Tinian, followed by Major Charles W. Sweeney in the **Great Artiste** and Captain George W. Marquardt in a third B-29. At 8:15am (local) the Little Boy type bomb was dropped on Hiroshima. The second and last atomic weapon dropped during World War II was of the Fat Man type. This weapon was dropped on Nagasaki by Major Sweeney flying **Bockscar.** The 509th BG was the only unit in the world capable of dropping a nuclear weapon at the end of the war.

The 509th Composite Group was reassigned to Roswell, New Mexico, after the war and could barely keep its airplanes in the air for routine proficiency due to the cutbacks after the war. On January 10, 1946, Colonel Paul T. Cullen was tasked with readying the 509th for Operation Crossroads as part of Vice Admiral W.H.P. Blandy's Task Force 1. Training for the 509th intensified in preparation for the forthcoming atomic bomb test in the Pacific. While scheduled for May 15th, the test was postponed until July 1st.

Numerous aircraft and ships were assigned to the task force, including the following B-29s:
- One B-29 command aircraft
- One B-29 bomb carrying aircraft **(Dave's Dream)**
- Two B-29 pressure drop aircraft
- Three B-29 weather reconnaissance aircraft
- Two B-29 (F-13) VLR radiological reconnaissance aircraft
- Eight F-13 VLR photographic aircraft
- One B-29 radio broadcast aircraft
- One B-29 press photography aircraft

All B-29s participating in Operation Crossroads were based at Kwajalein.

A variety of special mission instrumentation was installed on the various aircraft. A summary of this equipment for the B-29s follows:

B-29 BOMB CARRYING AIRPLANE

Equipment	Use
AN/APN-9 (Loran)	Normal.
SCR 718 (Altimeter)	Normal.
AN/ARN-7 (Compass)	Normal.
RC-103 (Inst. Landing)	Normal.
AN/ARN-5 (Inst. Landing)	Normal.
AN/ARCS	Transmit Bomb Away signal by tone only.
AN/ART-13	Transmit Bomb Away signal by voice and also used for running commentary.
ARC-3 (VHF)	On actual bombing run will transmit Bomb Away and running commentary simultaneously with AN/ART-13 above, on Button D (140.58 MCS). Will revert to normal use as soon as Bomb Away is given.
VHF Receiver (Extra)	Guards 140.58 MCS at all times.
SCR-695 (IFF)	
SCR-729 (Radar)	Homes on AN/CPN-6 Beacon for bombing run.

Suella J., F-13A, 44-62577, parked next to the vast array of cameras carried by the fleet of F-13s assigned to Operation Crossroads.

(USAF Museum)

F-13 PHOTOGRAPHIC AIRCRAFT

VHF Receiver (Extra)	Guards 140.58 MCS at all times.
AN/APN-9 (Loran)	Normal.
SCR 718 (Altimeter)	Normal.
AN/ARN-7 (Compass)	Normal.
RC-103 Instrument Landing	Normal.
AN/ARN-5 Instrument Landing	Normal.
SCR522 or AN/ARC-3 (VHF)	Normal.
AN/ART-13 (Liaison Transmitter)	Radiological Observers Net While in Target Area. Otherwise normal.
BC-348	
SCR 695 (IFF)	
AN/APQ-13 (Radar) & SCR-729 (Radar)	Equipped with scope cameras.

B-29 BROADCAST AIRCRAFT

Additional equipment will be added as required to provide:

1. Broadcast HF Channel one way to USS APPALACHIAN.
2. Q Channel one way USS APPALACHIAN to aircraft.
3. RATT Channel to USS APPALACHIAN.
4. Guard for Task Force Air Guard Channel.

B-29 COMMAND

Equipment	Use
Carries normal equipment. All equipment will have normal use except as noted below:	
AN/ARC-8 (Liaison)	Used by radiological observer.
VHF Receiver (Extra)	Guards 150.58 MCS at all times.

B-29 PRESSURE DROP

Carries same equipment as B-29 Bomb Carrying Airplane. All equipment will have normal use except as noted below:	
VHF Receiver (Extra)	Guards 140.58 MCS at all times.

B-29 PRESS PHOTO

Normal except extra HF receiver for Task Force Air Guard and AN/ART-13 Liaison - Radiological Observers Net while in Target Area:

Warm Front, B-29A-65-BN, 44-62128, was assigned to the 59th Reconnaissance Squadron (VLR) Weather, 311th Reconnaissance Wing. The name appears to be related to LTC Nick Chavasse, Commander of Task Group 1.57. During World War II he flew a B-24L-11-FO, 44-49534, with the 55th Reconnaissance Squadron (Long Range Weather). That ship was also named **Warm Front.**

(Larkins)

The mission of the Command Aircraft was to fly from Kwajalein to the vicinity of Bikini Atoll and maintain an altitude of 8,500 feet. The aircraft was to be on a non-interference orbit with other aircraft and maintain a twenty nautical mile distance from the target until the blast and then no closer than eight nautical miles after the blast. This aircraft provided appropriate reports to the Commander Joint Task Force -1 (CJTF-1).

The bomb carrying aircraft was to drop a nuclear weapon on a target in the ship target array in Bikini Atoll. This aircraft was to make three practice runs after which the bomb would be released on the fourth or fifth run at the bombardier's discretion. If unable to drop after the fifth run the aircraft was to return to base. The bomb run was executed at 200 mph. Upon bomb release, the aircraft would execute a 150° turn to the left, descending 1,000 feet, then maintain course and altitude for five minutes.

The Pressure Drop Aircraft would drop three parachute type condenser air blast gauges over Bikini Atoll in order to record the blast pressure from the detonation. These aircraft arrived on station at an altitude which was 1,000 feet below that of the bomb carrier. Their orbit, 180° apart, had a seven nautical mile slant range from the target and was flown in a counter-clockwise direction. Upon the bomb release signal from the bomber, the Pressure Drop Aircraft would release their blast gauges. Upon gauge release, these aircraft would execute a 90° turn to the right and descend 1,000 feet. This course would be maintained for five minutes.

The Weather Reconnaissance Aircraft performed tasks ordered by the CJTF-1. One aircraft, **Warm Front,** RB-29A-65-BN, 44-62128, departed Kwajalein at 2:15am and flew a 10 hour mission prior to the detonation. The

pilot was 1/Lt Frank A. Bagley.

The Radiological Reconnaissance Aircraft, one B-29 and one F-13, would track and photograph the blast cloud until darkness or until no longer visible in order to determine the persistance of the cloud and the radiological activity contained therein. These aircraft flew at 25,000 feet. The B-29 maintained a forty nautical mile distance from the target, while the F-13 flew thirty miles away. Thirty minutes after the blast, these aircraft rendezvoused forty miles from the target, then established an altitude separation of 500 feet. These aircraft then proceeded to track the cloud on opposite sides at a distance of thirty miles from the cloud.

The Photographic Aircraft, (F-13s), would photograph conditions in the Bikini Atoll before, during, and after detonation. One flight of four flew at 26,000 feet while the second flight of four maintained a 27,000 feet altitude. The first flight photographed vertically along the bomb run axis, then proceeded to orbit, equally spaced, in a circle 13.5 miles from the target, thus affording an approximate fifteen mile slant range. Following the blast, the first flight descended while maintaining an eight mile separation from the cloud for six minutes, then returned to base. The second flight stood by as spares for the first flight and photographed the bomber throughout its bomb run, the bomb throughout its fall, and the cloud development for four minutes after its development. The second flight then returned to base.

The Radio Broadcast Aircraft flew at 7,000 feet, maintained a twenty nautical mile separation from the target and broadcasted live for eighty-five minutes. Its orbit was flown in a counter-clockwise direction.

The Press Photography Aircraft flew at 4,000 feet maintaining a twenty mile counter-clockwise orbit. This

Sweet 'n' Lola, F-13A, 44-61578, usually carried the last four digits of the serial number on the nose. For Operation Crossroads, the 24-inch yellow band was applied to the aft fuselage and the last three digits of the serial number were added to the rear. The 10x10-foot black square with yellow F was applied to the vertical tail. *(Bowers)*

aircraft could remain on station for no more than thirty minutes.

The following markings were applied to the various B-29/F-13 aircraft participating in Operation Crossroads:

- Command Aircraft - no special markings.
- Bomb Carrying Airplane - A black 10x10 foot square with a large yellow B was applied to the tail. A pair of 24-inch wide bands, one black and one yellow, were applied to the fuselage just aft of the national insignia. The last three digits of the airplane number were applied in black just aft of the stripes. A pair of 24-inch wide bands, one black and one yellow, were applied to the wings just outboard of the outboard engines.
- Pressure Drop Aircraft - A black circle, 12 feet in diameter, enclosing a black arrow was applied to the vertical tail. A 24-inch wide red band was applied around the wings just outboard of the outboard engines. A 24-inch red band was applied just aft of the national insignia on the fuselage. The last three digits of the serial number were applied aft of the fuselage band.
- Weather Reconnaissance Aircraft - A black 10x10 foot square with a large yellow W was applied to the vertical tail.
- Radiological Reconnaissance Aircraft - no special markings.
- VLR Photographic Aircraft - A black 10x10 foot square with a large yellow F was applied to the vertical tail. A 24-inch wide yellow band was applied around the wings outboard of the outboard engines. A 24-inch wide yellow band was applied around the fuselage just aft of the national insignia. The last three digits of the serial number were applied aft of the

fuselage band.

The F-13 aircraft were modified to carry a number of cameras throughout the pressurized compartments, forward bomb bay and in the turret positions. These cameras were as follows:

- Jeromes in the turrets
- Eastman and Fastax motion picture cameras in the nose
- K-18 vertical and oblique cameras in the forward bomb bay and aft fuselage
- K-22 vertical camera in the aft fuselage

Modifications for the F-13s employed in Operation Crossroads were accomplished at the depot in Oklahoma City, Oklahoma.

The following modified aircraft participated in Operation Crossroads:

F-13A-35-BN	44-61577	**Suella J**
F-13A-35-BN	44-61578	**Sweet 'n' Lola**
F-13A-35-BN	44-61583	**Kamra-Kaze**
F-13A-50-BN	44-61822	**The Belle of Bikini**
F-13A-55-BN	44-61960	**Mary Lou**
F-13A-55-BN	44-61991	**The Angellic Pig**
F-13A-55-BN	44-61999	**Over Exposed**
F-13A-55-BN	44-62000	**Kamode Head**

Gauge Aircraft

| B-29-50-MO | 44-86436 |
| B-29-50-MO | 44-86383 |

Radiological Reconnaissance

| B-29-55-MO | 44-86384 |
| B-29-55-MO | 44-86430 |

F-13A, 44-61822, reveals the markings carried on the right side of the photographic aircraft. The 59th Bomb Wing insignia was applied to the forward fuselage.

(Bowers)

Dave's Dream, B-29-50-MO, 44-87354, flown by Major Woodrow P. Swaincutt, dropped a Fat Man-type atomic bomb on a fleet of seventy-three ships off the Bikini Atoll, on July 1, 1946. Mechanical problems precluded Colonel Paul Tibbets from making the drop in his **Enola Gay,** B-29-45-MO, 44-86292.

(USAF)

Kamode Head, F-13A, 44-62000, reveals the standard camera sight fairing under the nose.

(USAF Museum J4/US/AC/pho 54)

The Belle of Bikini was the name carried by F-13A, 44-61822. Mission markers in the form of cameras were painted on the nose.

(USAF Museum J4/US/AC/B-29/pho 45)

Kamra-Kaze, F-13A, 44-61583, like all of these aircraft, carried the Yagi antenna on the forward fuselage.

(USAF Museum J4/US/AC/B-29/pho 56)

F-13 PHOTOGRAPHIC AIRCRAFT CAMERA INSTALLATIONS

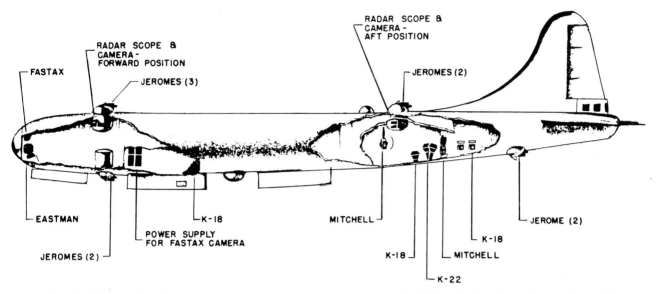

RADAR SCOPE &
CAMERA -
FORWARD POSITION

RADAR SCOPE &
CAMERA -
AFT POSITION

FASTAX

JEROMES (3)

JEROMES (2)

EASTMAN

K-18

MITCHELL

JEROME (2)

POWER SUPPLY
FOR FASTAX CAMERA

K-18

JEROMES (2)

K-18

MITCHELL

K-22

Above: Jerome cameras were carried in the turrets. Three of these units were installed in the upper forward turret. (USAF)

Left: Fastax and Eastman cameras were carried in the nose. (USAF)

The aft-most Mitchell motion picture camera was located on the left side of the airplane adjacent to the K-22 camera. (USAF)

A pair of K-18 cameras were mounted obliquely in the left side of the aft fuselage. (USAF)

9

SILVERPLATE & SADDLETREE

*The **Enola Gay** had its arrow replaced with an R in order to conceal its identity. All but the tail armament had been deleted. The scanner's blisters were removed and plugged.*   *(USAF)*

For Project A, a total of 17 Martin-Omaha-built B-29s were modified to carry the test shapes. British release mechanisms, then used for the 12,000-pound British bombs, were installed in the B-29s. These mechanisms required only a single lug on the bomb. Testing was conducted in the Wendover, Utah, area by the 216th AABU.

The first airplane modified to carry the shapes was B-29-5-BW, 42-6259. The installation was essentially mocked up on this airplane at Wright Field, Ohio, between December 1944 and January 1945.

Silverplate Project - The codename Silverplate was officially given to the aerial delivery portion of the atomic weapons program, and was initiated on December 1, 1944. Under Project 9814S, a total of seventeen Martin-Omaha B-29s was modified for testing. Subsequently, Project 98228S called for modification of an additional twenty-eight B-29s. The second lot had fuel injected engines, Curtis electric propellers, deletion of all but the tail armament, and revised bomb bays. Specific modifications included the following:

- New H-frame support
- C-6 bomb hoist
- Sway braces
- Carrier assembly
- Antenna installation
- Junction box
- British Type F release unit
- British Type G shackle assembly
- Winker-type bomb bay doors in lieu of the existing snap opening doors
- SCR-718 radio altimeter

Development of systems for atomic weapons fell into three programs: Project A, Silverplate, and Saddletree.

While the Manhattan Project was concerned with the development of the weapon technology, Project A covered the planning and testing for the eventual combat use of the weapons. Project A was not officially established until March 1945; however, studies of ballistic models and bomb component procurement were underway in 1944.

Project A - Three different bomb types were studied. These were:

- Little Boy - 23-inch diameter, 120-inch length, weighing 9,000 pounds. Contained a U^{235} gun assembly. (Also known as Mark II.)
- Fat Man Model 1222 - Discarded because of poor ballistics and a requirement for over 1500 bolts used in assembly.
- Fat Man Model 1561 - 60-inch diameter, 128-inch length, weighing 10,000 pounds. Employed an implosion detonation system. (Also known as Mark III - Mod. 0, or FM Mark III - Mod. 0.)

The 509th's insignia was a large circle and arrow in black on the vertical tail. As a means of disguising the group, they adopted a series of existing group tail markings. These were:

- 497th BG's A — 71, 72, 73, 84
- 444th BG's Triangle N — 77, 85, 86, 88
- 6th BG's Circle R — 82, 89, 90, 91
- 39th BG's Square P — 83, 94, 95

Flight tests were conducted between February 18, 1944, and November 1, 1944. The test sites included: Wendover AAB, Utah; Muroc AAFB, California; and Wright Field, Ohio. It is presumed that the prototype airplane was used in the development of the bomb racks

*The tail of **Bockscar** carried the spurious markings for the 444th Bomb Group. In the background is the **Enola Gay** with its correct circle and arrow insignia. See the color section for more details of **Bockscar**.* *(Levy)*

and delivery procedures. In addition to the USAAF, other organizations involved in these tests included: Manhattan Project, U.S. Navy, and the Sandia Corporation.

The only unit to drop an atomic weapon in combat was the 393rd BS, 509th Composite Group, under the command of Colonel Paul W. Tibbets, Jr. The aircraft assigned to the unit were as follows:

Block No.	Serial No.	Plane in Group No.	Name
B-29-35-MO	44-27296	84	-*
B-29-35-MO	44-27297	77	**Bockscar**
B-29-35-MO	44-27298	83	**Full House**
B-29-35-MO	44-27299	86	**Next Objective**
B-29-35-MO	44-27300	73	**Strange Cargo**
B-29-35-MO	44-27301	85	**Straight Flush**
B-29-35-MO	44-27302	72	**Top Secret**
B-29-35-MO	44-27303	71	**Jabbitt III**
B-29-35-MO	44-27304	88	**Up An' Atom****
B-29-40-MO	44-27353	89	**The Great Artiste**
B-29-40-MO	44-27354	90	**Big Stink****
B-29-45-MO	44-86291	91	**Necessary Evil**
B-29-45-MO	44-86292	82	**Enola Gay**
B-29-50-MO	44-86346	94	**Spook****
B-29-50-MO	44-86347	95	**Laggin' Dragon**

   * Not known to have gone overseas.
  ** Named after V-J Day.
*** Renamed **Dave's Dream** after V-J Day.

After World War II, the 509th's B-29s returned to the Oklahoma City Air Materiel Area for installation of an MX-344 radar computer, more easily removeable snap-ring engine cowls, and other miscellaneous items which would improve the performance of the airplanes.

In July 1946, the Sacramento Air Materiel Area was selected to continue the Silverplate modifications and incorporate the following additional changes:
• AN/APQ-13 radar
• Curtis electric propellers
• Fuel injected engines
• Fuel flow meter
• Winterization

The code name Silverplate was compromised on May 12, 1947, and the name was immediately changed to Saddletree.

With the development of American components, the British F and G mechanisms could be replaced. These changes included:
• Installation of the Type U-1 bomb rack
• Installation of the Type C-7 bomb hoist

A total of 3,469 manhours were required to accomplish the initial Silverplate modifications on each airplane. Subsequent changes in the design requirements resulted in the expenditure of 11,000 manhours per airplane.

Because of the differences between the Little Boy and Fat Man bombs, an adaptor kit for the Little Boy was provided for each airplane. The Fat Man-type was considered to be the standard bomb.

The Silverplate/Saddletree modifications would become the cornerstone of the post-war modernization program under the GEM Project.

GEM PROGRAM

The U.S. Strategic Bombing Survey, conducted after World War II, concluded that strategic air power had a limited effect on ending the war. While the bombers disrupted enemy production, their forces in the field had sufficient equipment to offer substantial resistance, according to the report. However, the survey neglected to capture the fact that the combined US/British day/night bombardment of Nazi Germany brought the horrors of war to the German people. This bombing tied up a great deal of the Nazi resources - factory workers, civil defense workers, anti-aircraft crews, fighter-interceptor personnel, all of whom could have been at the battle front to counter the Allied armies. In addition, such bombardment wore down the enemy's will to fight because of the lack of rest.

In the Pacific Theater it was later reported that a single earthquake in Japan wrecked more havoc than our bombers. However, the bombers did have an effect on the will of the enemy. Had the United States pursued an amphibious assault on the Japanese home islands, great bloodshed would have occurred on both sides. MG James H. Doolittle stated: "The Navy had the transport to make the invasion of Japan possible, the ground forces had the power to make it possible, and the B-29 made it unnecessary."

After World War II the Cold War went into effect. While the Soviet Union was overrunning Europe in a series of political coup d'etats, the U.S. Joint Chiefs of Staff (JCS) made plans to muster the desired deterrence. At the end of World War II, the USAAF, along with the other services, was drastically reduced. Units were disbanded and personnel were discharged to civilian life. While there was a surplus of pilots, there were few maintenance personnel. The JCS goal for a seventy-eight group air force had to be forgone. The USAAF opted for a seventy-group organization, with twenty-five groups dedicated to strategic bombardment. Initially, rehabilitation of this peacetime air force came with fifty-five groups. The seventy groups would have to come in a

second phase. In June of 1946, there were ten heavy bombardment groups, two of which were paper organizations. On March 21, 1946, three combat commands were established within the USAAF. These were Air Defense Command (ADC), Strategic Air Command (SAC), and Tactical Air Command (TAC). The B-29 had been selected as the mainstay of the bomber force. In 1946, 148 B-29s were in the inventory. By the following year this had increased to 319. In 1948, SAC had grown to 486 B-29s, 35 B-36s, and 35 B-50s. For the reconnaissance role SAC had gained 12 F-13s in 1947, while in 1948 this number had grown to 30 and the aircraft had been redesignated as RB-29s.

Upgrading of the bomber forces to meet the Cold War environment became a major program. The 509th BG, stationed at Roswell AAFld, New Mexico, possessed thirty of the air force's thirty-two atomic bomb-capable B-29s which had been modified to the Silverplate/Saddletree configuration. A total of 268 unmodified B-29s were in the SAC inventory when the Gem Program was initiated. In the summer of 1948, the JCS directed that 225 bombers be modified to have an atomic capability. The reason this capability was needed was that there was no way we could match the Soviet Union's forces man-for-man and tank-for-tank. For this very same reason our nation maintains a strong nuclear deterrent force today. The airplanes covered under the Saddletree program included B-29s, B-36s, and B-50s. The overall Gem Program included: Winterization, Superman, Ruralist, and Saddletree programs. Implementation of the Gem Project would permit global operations of all of the very heavy bombers in SAC's inventory and would provide one group of B-29s for Alaskan operations, complete with special electronic requirements. A summary of these modifications follows:

- Winterization. Modifications would permit operations to be conducted when the temperatures were as low as -65° F. Nesa glass and windshield de-icing provisions were made. Specialized electronics were

The Mk II Little Boy was of the type detonated over Hiroshima. It weighed 9,000 pounds and had the yield of about 20,000 tons of high explosives.

(USAF 164707AC)

The Mk III Fat Man was of the type detonated over Naga-saki. It weighed 10,000 pounds and had the yield of 20,000 tons of high explosives. This bomb became America's first standard nuclear weapon. (USAF 164708AC)

SILVERPLATE & SADDLETREE NOSE ART

Top Secret was flown by Captain Charles McKnight. A tally for dropping six Fat Man shapes is shown on the nose. (USAF)

Strange Cargo had dropped four Fat Man Shapes before going to Tinian. Lt Joseph Westover was the pilot. (USAF)

Straight Flush also dropped six Fat Man shapes. Captain Claude Eatherly was the pilot. (USAF)

Next Objective, flown by Lt. Ralph DeVore, had made four Fat Man practice drops. (USAF)

The Great Artiste appears to have dropped four Fat Man practice shapes, and had flown on two real missions - Hiroshima and Nagasaki, as the observation ship. The pilots for this aircraft were Lt. Charles Albury and Major Charles Sweeney. (USAF)

Full House had dropped a total of six Fat Man shapes. Captain Ralph Taylor was the pilot. (USAF)

Laggin' Dragon was flown by Captain Edward Costello. (USAF)

Necessary Evil, with four Fat Man practice drops to her credit, was flown by Lt. Norman Ray. (USAF)

installed in the Alaska-destined B-29s. A total of fifteen B-29s were scheduled for this modification by September 1, 1948. An additional eighty were to be completed by December 15, 1948.

- Superman. These were modifications for B-29s destined to become tankers. The changes included:
  - Deletion of all non-essential equipment
  - Self-sealing fuel cells replaced by non-self-sealing nylon cells for weight savings
  - Large capacity, single bomb bay tanks installed
  - AN/APQ-13 radar installed
  - Main gear tires replaced with B-50-type tires
  - Refueling equipment installed

- AN/APN-11 radar beacon installed

A total of forty TB-29s were scheduled for completion by December 15, 1948, and another eighty-four by January 1, 1949, or as soon as possible.

- Ruralist. These modifications were for B-29s destined to become receivers. The changes included:
  - Saddletree modifications
  - Single-point, manifold fuel systems installed for in-flight refueling
  - AN/APN-11 radar beacon installed

A total of forty-four B-29s were scheduled for the Ruralist modification, with no deadline set.

This H-frame, with four hoist motors, was installed in the bomb bay to raise the bomb into position. (USAF)

Close-up details of one of the hoist motors. (Los Alamos National Laboratory)

The bomb carrier and sway braces for the Little Boy. (Los Alamos National Laboratory)

General view of the bomb bay, looking up and forward. (USAF)

14

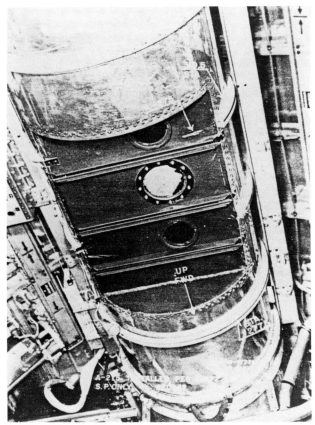

View looking up and forward of the reworked tunnel which provides room for the H-frame.

(Los Alamos National Laboratory)

Bomb bay antenna mounted on the aft face of the pressure bulkhead at the forward end of the forward bomb bay.

(Los Alamos National Laboratory)

This electrical junction box was installed in the upper left side of the bomb bay.

(Los Alamos National Laboratory)

Weapon operator's station located in the aft pressurized compartment.

(USAF)

Weapon operator's station with flight test box installed.

(Los Alamos National Laboratory)

TARZON BOMB CARRIERS

B-29-97-BW, 45-21748, was modified for use as a Tarzon bomb carrier by the Air Proving Ground Command at Eglin AFB. The blown B-50 nose piece is shown in this view, as is the relocated AN/APQ-13 radome. Normally the radome was centered between the bomb bay doors. This airplane was equipped with Curtiss electric propellers. During the Korean Conflict this airplane was used by the 19th Bomb Group. *(USAF 48979AC)*

The VB-13 Tarzon bomb (later redesignated (Y)ASM-A-1A) was a Bell Aircraft-built variation of the British 12,000-pound "Tallboy". This bomb was carried semi-internally, and was a free-falling weapon which could be guided both in range and azimuth. The bomb was 20.4 feet in length and had a 54-inch diameter lift shroud added around the center of gravity and an octagonal shroud with control surfaces added near the tail. This project was initiated on February 26, 1945. Tarzon bombs were to be used against targets requiring deep penetration and very heavy explosives such as battleships, concrete fortifications and structures, caves and other underground installations, dams and dikes, and landslides considered to be suitable targets. Use of the Tarzon was limited to days with excellent visibility. The aircraft had to remain on the bomb run until the bomb struck the target.

The guidance system consisted of an AN/ARW-38 radio transmitter in the launch aircraft and an AN/URW-2 radio set in the bomb. A flare was installed in the tail of the bomb to assist the bombardier in guiding the bomb. The M-series bombsight was modified so that it was possible to see a superimposed image of both the flare and the target. Roll stabilization was accomplished by ailerons mounted in the tail of the bomb. Range and azimuth were controlled by a set of elevators in the bomb tail. An electrical servo system in the bomb actuated the elevators and ailerons in response to radio signals from the launch aircraft.

Several modifications were made on the B-29s in order to accommodate the Tarzon bomb. The fuselage section between the bomb bay doors was removed, and the bomb bay doors were cut to conform to the cross section of the bomb. Modifications were made to the

bomb racks in order to support the weight at the individual shackles. The guidance system radio, antenna, and controller were added to the airplane. Lastly, the standard B-29 glazed nose piece was replaced by a blown plexiglass nose piece from a B-50 in order to afford the bombardier a better view of the bomb and its flare.

During the autumn of 1950, B-29s of the Far East Air Forces (FEAF) made bombing runs at 10,000 feet without fear of enemy air opposition. Each Superfortress dropped an average of four bombs per run over bridge targets, resulting in FEAF Bomber Command computations for 13.3 runs to destroy an "average" bridge. While not quite up to the accuracy standards expected, they were running through their assigned bridge targets so rapidly that it did not matter. With the arrival of the MiG-15s the B-29s were driven to 21,000 feet for their bombing runs and were only able to make one pass on a target. To improve their results over the target, the B-29s began dropping 2,000-pound bombs. In March 1951, an experimental mission was flown by the 19th BG with one formation dropping 4,000-pound light-case bombs with proximity fusing to determine the blast effect on the bridges. The results were not worthwhile.

In the autumn of 1950, a technical team from the Air Proving Ground Command worked with the 19th BG in testing the 1,000-pound Razon bombs. This World War II bomb had remotely controlled tail fins which responded to radio commands from the bombardier. Early malfunctions resulted in 331 of 487 (67 percent) responding to control commands. However, the last 150 Razon bombs dropped had a 97 percent reliability and fifteen bridges were destroyed. It took about four bombs to destroy an "average" bridge. In December 1950, the

The Bell Aircraft-built Tarzon bomb was photographed in a loading pit at Holloman AFB, New Mexico, in May 1949. The black and white paint scheme was for photographic purposes during the test program.
(USAF 46929AC)

The octagonal shroud had four fixed and four moveable sides. Four struts supported the shroud. Servo linkages moved the control surfaces. (USAF 46926AC)

19th BG changed over to the new Tarzon bomb. Of the initial ten bombs dropped, only one scored a hit. By March 1951, the 19th BG became quite skilled in the use of the Tarzons. FEAFs bombers had destroyed all of their bridge targets by this time, but the enemy quickly built by-pass spans and repaired the damaged bridges. Technical problems with the Tarzons continued. On March 29, three Tarzon-equipped B-29s were assigned to bomb the Sinuiju bridges. One aircraft returned to base with mechanical problems, a second aircraft with Colonel Payne Jennings, 19th BG commander, ditched at sea and exploded, and the third aircraft continued on to the target only to have the Tarzon miss the bridge. Thus ended the Tarzon program.

Three Superfortresses known to have been equipped for carrying the Tarzon bombs were B-29-97-BWs, serial numbers 45-21745, 45-21746, and 45-21748.

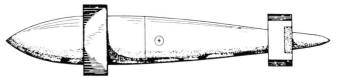

1/72nd SCALE DRAWING

OVERALL LENGTH 252"
BOMB DIAMETER 38"
LIFT SHROUD
DIAMETER 54"
CHORD 20"

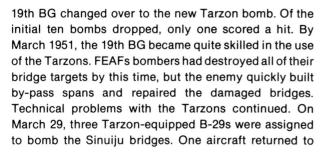

This Tarzon bomb is attached to its specially designed loading dolly. The support struts for the lift shroud are evident in this view. The photograph was taken at Eglin AFB, Florida, in October 1951. (USAF B-48979AC)

Side view of the Tarzon bomb on its loader.
(USAF A-48979AC)

With the airplane parked over the loading pit, the dolly-mounted bomb was positioned into the bomb bay. In this photograph, the aft bomb bay door had been removed. The contoured forward door is visible. A flare was installed in the hole in the tail cone fairing.

(USAF 48989AC)

The Tarzon bomb bomb rack and loading chain are revealed in this view of a test bomb at Holloman AFB in October 1949. *(USAF 46931AC)*

The ground clearance with the bomb installed is clearly evident in this view. *(USAF 46935AC)*

The contoured bomb bay doors may be seen in this view. The airplane is parked over an alignment stripe which leads to the loading pit seen to the rear.

(USAF 48979AC)

B-29-97-BW, 45-21746, is shown parked in a revetment on Okinawa in May 1951. This was one of the Tarzon bomb carriers. These anti-aircraft gunners were representative of the airfield defense. This airplane had a black belly and black band on the fin. The Indian head on the tail is indicative of the 19th Bomb Group's 93rd Bomb Squadron, making the fin cap, overwing life raft doors, wingtips, and nose band red. *(USAF G-1188-1)*

The score on 45-21746 is shown here - 2 MiGs, 2 Purple Hearts, 5 Razon bombing missions, and 12 Tarzon missions. *(USAF)*

TB-29

TB-29A-45-BN, 44-61748, served with the 307th Bomb Group in Korea, as identified by the remains of the Square Y on the vertical tail. This airplane subsequently served as a target tug. The distinctive red stripes may be seen on top of the wings and horizontal tail. This photograph was taken at China Lake as the airplane was being readied for its flight to the Imperial War Museum collection at RAF Duxord.   *(Naval Weapons Center 210216)*

The TB-29 designation was given to Superfortresses converted to a non-tactical configuration and usually employed in some training role. Some of these airplanes were used strictly for crew training, and carried additional seats for instructor/observers. A number of the TB-29s were equipped with a tow target system. When in the tow target configuration, bomb bay fuel tanks could not be installed because of the target reels. While the bombing equipment was retained, all defensive armament was removed. The tail compartment, formerly occupied by the tail gunner, was open at the aft end and therefore was unpressurized.

The tow target system consisted of a hydraulic power system, an electrical power system, tow reels, guide rollers and tubing, electro-hydraulic cable cutters, target pods, and a tow reel operator's control console located at the right scanner's position. The tow reel units were installed in the aft bomb bay. Each reel was powered by a reversible hydraulic motor and had 6500 feet of 3/16-inch diameter armored cable. The cable was routed through guide tubes on the outside of the fuselage to the tail of the airplane. The pair of modified Mark VIII reels were equipped with a level wind which guided the cable in or out, a clutch lever used to disengage the drum for ground operations, a brake band assembly used to stop rotation of the drum, and a positive lock assembly used to lock the drum for extended periods. The targets could be released electrically. In the event of an emergency, a pair of emergency release cables, one for each target, were located on each side and forward of the tail compartment.

TB-29s so equipped were assigned to tow target squadrons which operated in support of fighter units. In addition, they supported U.S. Army anti-aircraft units. Other aircraft used for this mission were the Douglas B-26 and North American B-45. The TB-29s served in the tow target role between 1951-1957. Within CONUS, the 9th AF performed the tow target mission, while in Europe it was done by the 12th AF. Alaskan Air Command also

had a squadron. These units were as follows:

9th AF	12th AF
1st TTS	5th TTS
2nd TTS	7155th TTS
3rd TTS	
4th TTS	**Alaskan Air Command**
	15th TTS

Tow target TB-29 markings appeared to be a series of twelve-inch red stripes applied as follows:
- 3 around the aft fuselage
- 2 across the top of each horizontal stabilizer
- 7 across the top of each wing

In addition, the wing tips, fin tip, and horizontal stabilizer tips were red. Arctic trim, when applied, took precedence over the tow target stripes on the outboard wing panels and empannage.

TB-29s were also modified for the radar calibration/ evaluation role. Air Defense Command employed these airplanes to check the capabilities of their detection and interceptor units. USAF units known to have operated the TB-29 in this role were:

    5th RCF
  107th RCF
4713th REF
4754th REF
5015th REF
  10th RCS

RCF = Radar Calibration Flight
REF = Radar Evaluation ECM Flight
RCS = Radar Calibration Squadron

The 4713th REF operated eight TB-29s from Griffis AFB, New York. Each airplane carried a name. One was **Snow White,** while the remaining seven were each named for one of the seven dwarfs.

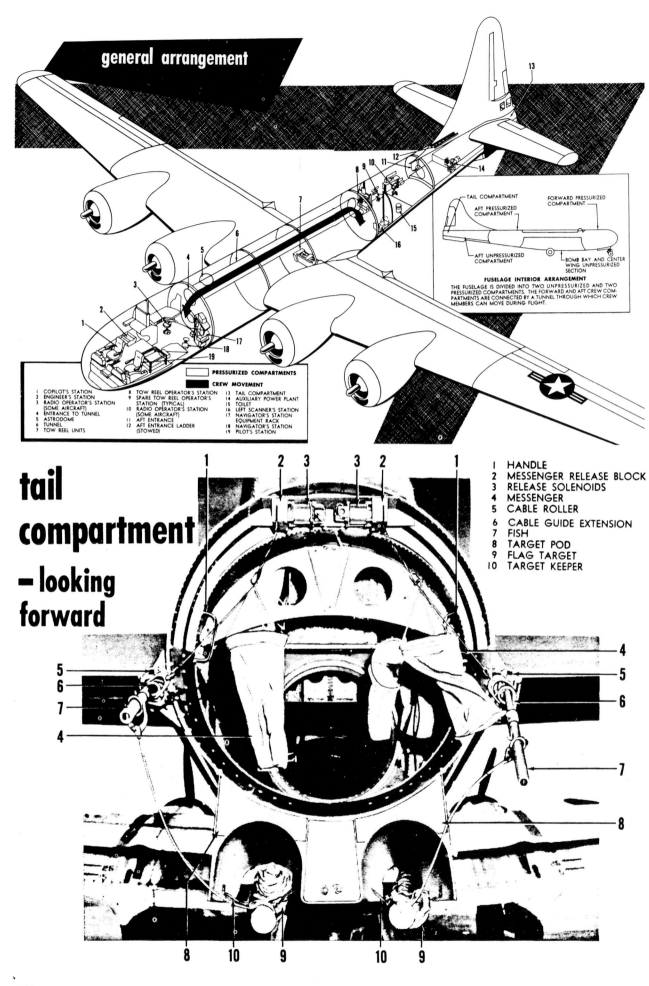

general arrangement

FUSELAGE INTERIOR ARRANGEMENT
THE FUSELAGE IS DIVIDED INTO TWO UNPRESSURIZED AND TWO PRESSURIZED COMPARTMENTS. THE FORWARD AND AFT CREW COMPARTMENTS ARE CONNECTED BY A TUNNEL THROUGH WHICH CREW MEMBERS CAN MOVE DURING FLIGHT.

TAIL COMPARTMENT
AFT PRESSURIZED COMPARTMENT
AFT UNPRESSURIZED COMPARTMENT
FORWARD PRESSURIZED COMPARTMENT
BOMB BAY AND CENTER WING UNPRESSURIZED SECTION

☐ PRESSURIZED COMPARTMENTS
■ CREW MOVEMENT

1 COPILOT'S STATION
2 ENGINEER'S STATION
3 RADIO OPERATOR'S STATION (SOME AIRCRAFT)
4 ENTRANCE TO TUNNEL
5 ASTRODOME
6 TUNNEL
7 TOW REEL UNITS
8 TOW REEL OPERATOR'S STATION
9 SPARE TOW REEL OPERATOR'S STATION (TYPICAL)
10 RADIO OPERATOR'S STATION (SOME AIRCRAFT)
11 AFT ENTRANCE
12 AFT ENTRANCE LADDER (STOWED)
13 TAIL COMPARTMENT
14 AUXILIARY POWER PLANT
15 TOILET
16 LEFT SCANNER'S STATION
17 NAVIGATOR'S STATION EQUIPMENT RACK
18 NAVIGATOR'S STATION
19 PILOT'S STATION

tail compartment
– looking forward

1 HANDLE
2 MESSENGER RELEASE BLOCK
3 RELEASE SOLENOIDS
4 MESSENGER
5 CABLE ROLLER
6 CABLE GUIDE EXTENSION
7 FISH
8 TARGET POD
9 FLAG TARGET
10 TARGET KEEPER

Above: TB-29-90-BW, 45-21740, was assigned to the 15th TTS based at Elmendorf AFB, Alaska, when photographed in September 1956. The three twelve-inch wide red waist bands and target sleeve shroud under the tail gunner's position identify the airplane as a target tug.
(USAF K17080)

Left: Tow target operator's control panel located at the right scanner's station. (Korade)

Horizontal stabilizer markings. (Korade)

Aft fuselage of TB-29-25-MO, 42-65281, reveals the target shroud and aft fuselage stripes. (Korade)

KB-29 HOSE TANKERS

Hose refueling is demonstrated by these 509th Bomb Group Superfortresses. The receiver carried the distinctive 509th arrow and circle tail marking, while the tanker had a triangle. Later the triangle would contain the letter C.

(Boeing 38524 via Williams)

The Strategic Air Command urgently needed to expand its operational capabilities during the latter half of the 1940s. During 1948, Boeing had reopened its Wichita Plant 2 in order to modify B-29s to the tanker configuration utilizing the hose system previously developed by Flight Refueling, Limited, of Great Britain. In addition to the refueling system, a 2,300 gallon jettisonable fuel tank was installed in each bomb bay, resulting in a 12,032 gallon useable fuel capacity. With this modification, the airplanes were redesignated KB-29M. A total of ninety-two of these conversions were made.

A hose windlass and refueling panel were added to the aft fuselage above the aft lower turret. Refueling operations were conducted as follows:

- The receiver aircraft would establish a heading and altitude. The tanker would formate approximately twenty feet above the receiver, offset to the left, and ten to twenty feet to the rear. The receiver played out a receiving line with a drag cone and pawl grapnel attached. The tanker trailed a contact line with a sinker weight attached.
- A cross-over maneuver was accomplished. The tanker slowly moved to the right of the receiver, then fell back until the pawl grapnel engaged the contact line. The tanker then pulled forward and reeled in the contact line.
- The aircraft achieved a formation in which there was a sixty foot vertical separation, with the tanker still above, and the tanker's nose aft and twenty feet to the right of the receiver's right wingtip. The hauling line was drawn into the tanker and attached to the refueling hose nozzle. The hose was then played out from the tanker and drawn into the receiver coupling by the receiver. Toggles were engaged, fuel valves were opened, and the fuel transfer pumps were turned on, thus enabling the transfer of fuel.
- While maintaining formation, the tanker would reel in the refueling hose and hauling line. The refueling operator detached the bayonet coupler from the hose nozzle and attached the drag cone and pawl grapnel to the hauling line.

The crew complement of the KB-29M was: pilot, copilot, flight engineer, navigator, radio operator, left scanner, and radar operator. The left scanner manned the refueling station during in-flight refueling operations.

A total of seventy-two Superfortresses were modified into receivers and were designated as B-29MRs. These aircraft had a maximum fuel capacity of 9,349 gallons with the addition of an aft bomb bay tank. All turrets and guns, except the tail gun position, were deleted on the B-29MRs. An auxiliary crew member's station was added in lieu of the former radio operator's position. The new position was in the aft unpressurized compartment. The B-29MR, as a consequence, had half the bomb carrying capacity of a standard B-29. During refueling operations, all fuel was directed into the aft bomb bay fuel tank and then ported to other tanks through the normal fuel transfer system. The initial designation for these airplanes was B-29L.

Both the KB-29Ms and B-29MRs were modified to incorporate the AN/APN-2B and AN/APN-68 radios for rendezvous.

Homogonized Ethyl, KB-29M-60-BW, 44-69710, flew with the 43rd ARefS. The blue and white aft fuselage band was another distinctive feature of the unit's markings. *(Larkins)*

Gracious Oasis, KB-29M-90-BW, 44-87747, was assigned to the 2nd ARefS, 2nd BG, stationed at Hunter AFB, Georgia. The 2nd BG was assigned to the 8th AF as indicated by the insignia on the fin and the diamond group marking. *(Boeing P9694)*

KB-29M-50-BW, 44-69704, demonstrates the hose and drogue refueling method with an F-86. *(Williams)*

Sky Octane, was B-29M-90-BW, 45-21716, assigned to the 43rd ARefS, 43rd BG, based at Davis-Monthan AFB. A circle K was carried on the tail along with the 15th AF insignia. Blue and white trim was applied to the nose gear doors and fin cap. *(Williams)*

KB-29M GENERAL ARRANGEMENT

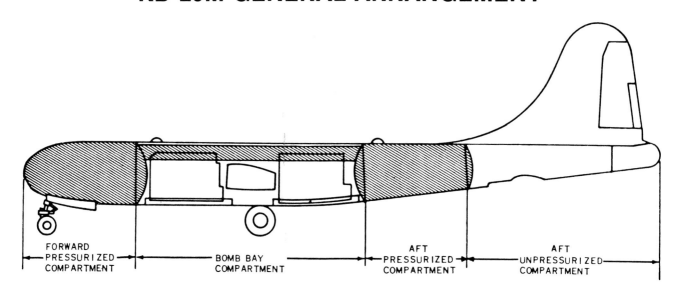

FORWARD PRESSURIZED COMPARTMENT — BOMB BAY COMPARTMENT — AFT PRESSURIZED COMPARTMENT — AFT UNPRESSURIZED COMPARTMENT

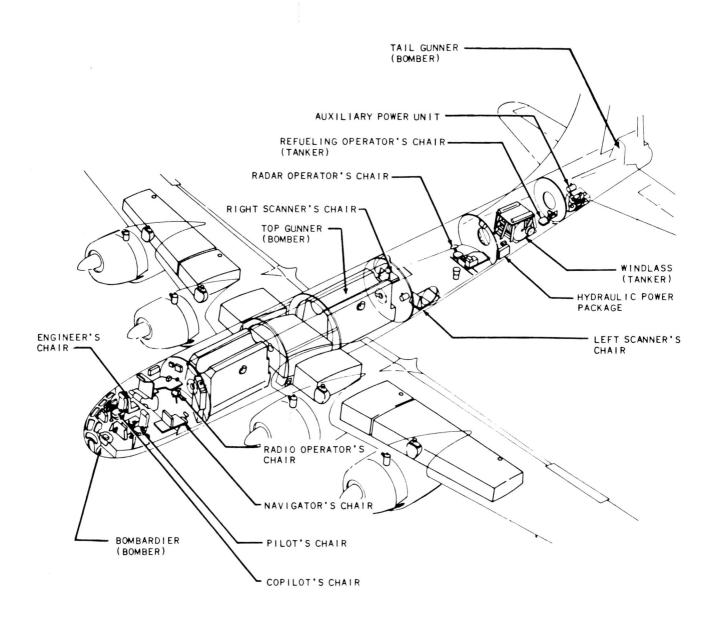

TAIL GUNNER (BOMBER)

AUXILIARY POWER UNIT

REFUELING OPERATOR'S CHAIR (TANKER)

RADAR OPERATOR'S CHAIR

RIGHT SCANNER'S CHAIR

TOP GUNNER (BOMBER)

WINDLASS (TANKER)

HYDRAULIC POWER PACKAGE

LEFT SCANNER'S CHAIR

ENGINEER'S CHAIR

RADIO OPERATOR'S CHAIR

NAVIGATOR'S CHAIR

BOMBARDIER (BOMBER)

PILOT'S CHAIR

COPILOT'S CHAIR

24

KB-29M-40-MO, 44-27329, of the 421st ARefS, was photographed over Japan on August 13, 1956. The unit was known as the "Rainbow Squadron" because of its colorful markings.   *(USAF 9251AC)*

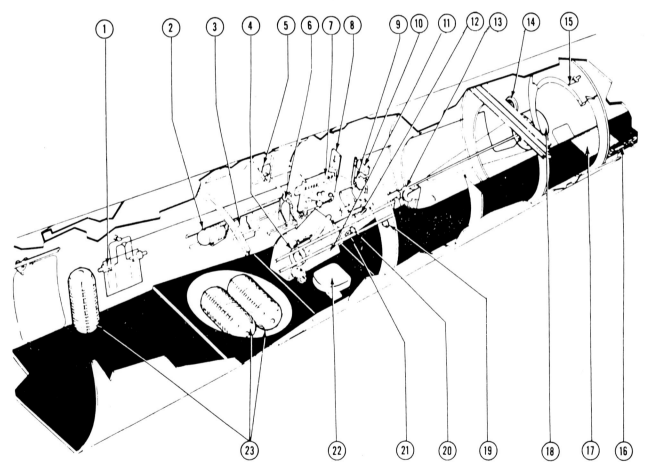

REFUELING EQUIPMENT

1 RECEIVER COUPLING PURGING CYLINDERS(2)
2 CO_2 HAND FIRE EXTINGUISHER
3 DOME LIGHTS(3)
4 THREADING LINE
5 INTERPHONE JACK BOX
6 PORTABLE OXYGEN BOTTLE
7 REFUELING OPERATOR'S PANEL
8 SUIT HEATER RECEPTACLE AND RHEOSTAT
9 OXYGEN REGULATOR
10 OXYGEN FLOW METER
11 HAULING LINE WINDLASS
12 CABLE ACCESS DOOR LAMP

13 CABLE GUIDE PULLEY
14 SPARE HAULING LINE AND REEL
15 SCREWDRIVER
16 CROOKS(2)
17 DRAG CONE AND PAWL GRAPNEL STOWAGE
18 RECEIVER COUPLING
19 EMERGENCY ALARM BELL
20 WIRE CUTTER
21 CABLE ACCESS DOOR
22 REFUELING OPERATOR'S CHAIR
23 OXYGEN CYLINDERS(3)

YB-29J

B-29-55-MO, 44-86398, was converted into a boom-type tanker. An F-84G-1-RE, 51-787, hooks up during a test flight.
(Williams)

Five non-tactical Superfortresses were modified by the Curtiss-Wright Corporation and designated YB-29Js. Higher powered R-3350-79 engines were installed with Curtiss electric C6445-B312 synchronized, fast-feathering, fast-reversing propellers. All armament provisions except the tail turret were deleted. These aircraft were:

B-29-55-MO	44-86398
B-29-55-MO	44-86402
B-29A-60-BN	44-62027
KB-29M-40-MO	44-27349
TB-29B-60-BA	44-84061

All of these aircraft, except the KB-29M, (44-27349), were equipped with the AN/APQ-13 bomb/nav radar and AN/APN-4 navigational radar, while the KB-29M had the AN/APN-2B and AN/APN-68 rendezvous equipment.

The "Andy Gump" nacelles, intended for use on the B-29As, were service evaluated on the YB-29Js. This distinctive cowl had the oil cooler intake set back under the aft edge of the cowl.

Two of the B-29s, 44-86398 and 44-86402, would become prototype boom tankers. At a point in time some of the aircraft were redesignated RB-29J, the R standing for restricted. TB-29B-60-BA, 44-84061, named **Dreamboat,** would eventually be a world's record setter.

Named **Dreamboat,** 44-84061 set an 8,193-mile non-stop record when it flew from Guam to Washington, D.C., in thirty-five hours, three minutes, on November 19, 1945. A previous record of 7,158 miles had been held by Great Britain. On December 11, 1945, the same airplane broke a record from Burbank, California, to Floyd Bennett Field, New York, making the 2,454-mile flight in five hours, twenty-seven minutes, averaging 450 mph. The previous record of six hours, thirty-one minutes, averaging 378.5 mph, was held by a P-51 Mustang. Both B-29 flights were flown with Col. C. S. Irvine in command.

The airplane was renamed **PACUSAN Dreamboat,** for Pacific Air Command, United States Army. The aircraft was greatly modified at Oklahoma City. In November 1945, the aircraft, under command of Col. Irvine, made a 10,000-mile non-stop flight from Oahu, Hawaii, to Cairo, Egypt, with the route passing over the North Pole. This flight was accomplished in thirty-nine hours, thirty-six minutes.

Belly stripes and director lights appear on the bomb bay door.
(Williams)

This was one of two YB-29Js modified into a boom type-tanker. This aircraft was fitted with cuffed Curtiss electric propellers. The photograph dates from May 1951. (Williams)

This view of 44-86402, shows the cowls to good effect. (Williams)

44-86402 reveals a stiffener extending rearward from the aft bomb bay door cutout. (Williams)

PACUSAN DREAMBOAT

This front view of the **PACUSAN Dreamboat** reveals the "Andy Gump" cowls and the three-bladed propellers.
(Williams)

The auxiliary power plant door was open when this picture was taken over the Seattle area.
(Boeing 6224)

The **PACUSAN Dreamboat,** 44-84061, was subsequently assigned to the newly-formed Strategic Air Command. It is seen here replete with a SAC "Milky way" band around the waist and the then extant SAC insignia on the fin.
(Williams)

The crew of the **PACUSAN Dreamboat.**
(Williams)

KB-29P BOOM TANKER

B-29-50-MO, 44-86363, was converted to a KB-29P. It was photographed while refueling an RB-45C-NA, serial number 48-012. RB-45s served with the 91st SRS both within the Continental United States and in Korea. (via Williams)

Refueling by the hose and drogue method employed by the KB-29M was tedious, time consuming, and slow. Experience showed that there had to be a better method, so Boeing developed the flying boom. While initially developed for use on the B-29, this same boom, with improvements, has been employed on the KC-97 Stratofreighter and the KC-135 Stratotanker. In addition, later versions of this boom were used on the KC-707s and 747s delivered to the Imperial Iranian Air Force and the KE-3As for the Royal Saudi Air Force.

The KB-29P flying boom tanker was a non-tactical version of the standard B-29 heavy bombardment aircraft. All defensive armament was deleted and an air refueling system was installed. A telescoping boom was attached to a hinged joint on the aft lower fuselage and controlled by a boom operator located in the former tail gunner's station. The aircraft's fuel system was modified to include a manifold system for normal engine operation, and a high capacity system for inflight refueling operations. Controls for these systems permitted the flight engineer to transfer a major portion of the tanker's fuel in the four wing tanks, or all of the fuel in the center section and bomb bay tanks, to the receiver.

Being a non-combat aircraft, all tanks on the tanker were made up of nylon non-self-sealing cells. While the maximum fuel capacity for a B-29 bomber was 9,363 gallons, the KB-29P carried 11,954 gallons. Initially, all fuel tanks were serviced with Mil-F-5572, grade 100/130 or 115/145 aviation gasoline. When the KB-29Ps were subsequently used to refuel jet aircraft, the aviation gasoline was restricted to the four main wing tanks and the two bomb bay tanks, while wing center section tanks were serviced with Mil-F-5624 (JP-4) jet fuel.

Refueling operations were conducted by precise formation flying and coordinated crew activities. A summary of the refueling operations follows:

- KB-29P assumes a cruise attitude. The boom operator extends the boom.
- Receiver aircraft moves into position below and behind the tanker using alignment bands on the tanker for reference. Receiver opens receptacle.
- Boom operator guides boom into receptacle. Coordination between boom operator and flight engineer directs fuel into the receiver.
- As weights of the two aircraft change (decrease in tanker and increase in receiver) and center-of-gravity changes, the receiver pilot uses the indicator lights for minor attitude adjustments required to maintain position. The lights read: RIGHT, LEFT UP, DWN, FWD, and AFT.
- Upon completion of refueling, the receiver drops off the boom. The boom operator purges the refueling manifold with nitrogen to prevent an explosion of the trapped fuel.

The normal crew complement on the KB-29P was: pilot, copilot, flight engineer, navigator, radio operator, two scanners, radar operator, and boom operator.

A contract for initial conversion of bombers to boom tankers was submitted in November 1949. For security reasons this fact was not made public until April 4, 1950, when the USAF confirmed that refueling tests had been conducted between a boom-equipped tanker and an F-84. These tests were conducted in the Seattle area.

A test of night refueling was conducted by KB-29Ps from the 307th Air Refueling Squadron, 307th BW, stationed at MacDill AFB, Florida, and F-84Gs from the 27th Fighter Escort Wing, based at Bergstrom AFB, Texas. The tests were conducted during the night of July 16, 1952. Two KB-29Ps and twenty-four F-84Gs were involved in the exercise. A total of eighty-four contacts were made with thirty-four of them being wet contacts. A total of 17,000 pounds of fuel was transferred, which averaged approximately 500 pounds per wet contact. The fastest hookup time was seven seconds, while the longest was ten minutes. The average was thirteen seconds. The time was measured from when the fighters closed from a position fifty feet behind the tanker to when contact was made. The refuelings took place in the vicinity of Bergstrom, and were conducted at an altitude of 10,000 feet between the hours of 8:30pm and 11:00pm.

Two major fighter deployments were made in 1952 using refueling support from KB-29Ps. The first was "Fox Peter One", conducted in early July, when a total of fifty-eight F-84Gs from the 31st Fighter Escort Wing were flown from Turner AFB, Georgia, to Misawa and Chitose Air Bases, Japan. Col. David C. Schilling, 31st FEW Commander, led the mission. Tankers from the 2nd and 91st Air Refueling Squadrons serviced the fighters on the first leg of the trip from Turner to Travis AFB, California. The second leg was from Travis to Hickham AFB, Hawaii, with service being provided by tankers from the 2nd, 91st, and 93rd ARefSs. From Hickham to Japan, the fighters island-hopped with stops at Midway, Wake, Eniwetok, Guam and Iwo Jima. For accomplishments on this 10,919-mile flight, the 31st FEW was awarded the Air Force Outstanding Unit Award.

When the 27th FEW, stationed at Bergstrom AFB, Texas, was selected to replace the 31st FEW in Japan, under a ninety-day rotational program, "Fox Peter Two" was conducted in October 1952. Under the command of Col. Donald J. Blakeslee, the 27th FEW deployed seventy-five F-84Gs over 7,800 miles. The trip was conducted between October 3 and October 14, 1952. Refueling service was provided by tankers from the 91st, 93rd, and 509th ARefSs.

KB-29P EQUIPMENT DIAGRAM

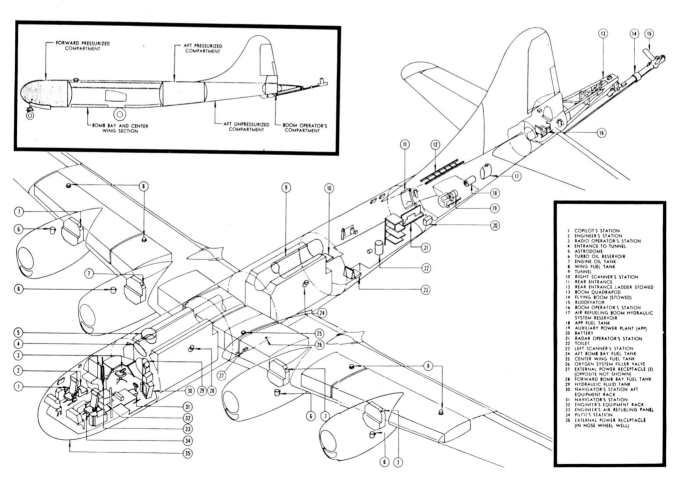

KB-29P

3-VIEW DRAWING

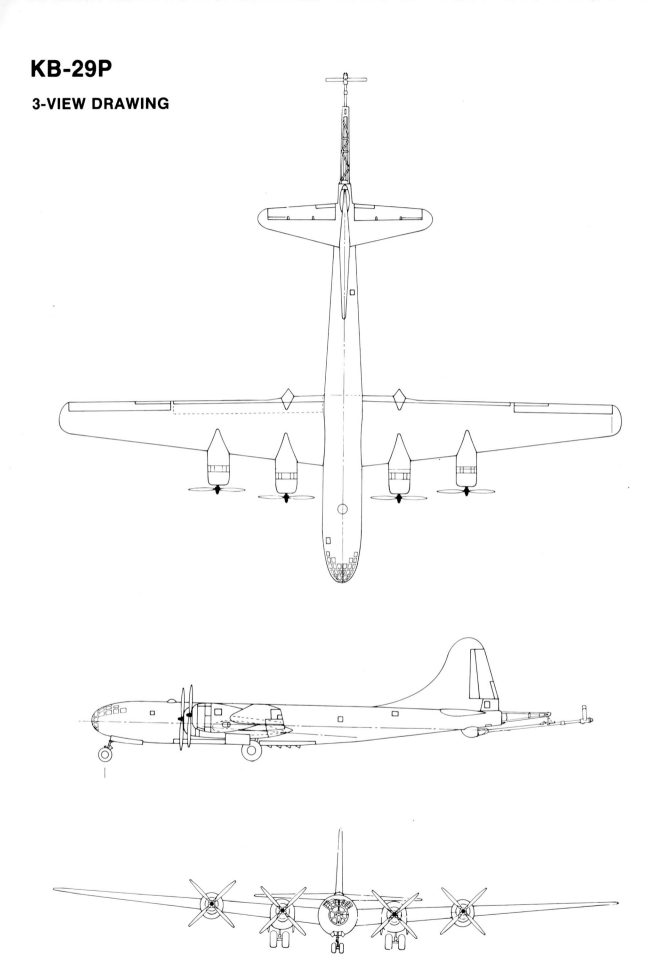

A total of 116 KB-29P conversions were made at the Boeing-Renton Plant.

Between the years of 1950 and 1957, SAC operated KB-29Ps in as many as ten air refueling squadrons with twenty aircraft per unit. A summary of these units is in the following table.

Unit	Base	Years	Markings
2nd ARefS, 2nd BW	Hunter AFB, GA	1951-1953	Square
9th ARefS, 9th BW	Mountain Home AFB, ID	1953	-
27th ARefS, 27th FEW	Bergstrom AFB, TX	1953-1955	
43rd ARefS, 43rd BW	Carswell AFB, TX	1949-1955	Circle K
91st ARefS, 91st SRW	Barksdale AFB, LA/	1950-1951	Square I
	Lockbourne AFB, OH	1951-1953	Circle X
93rd ARefS, 93rd BW	Castle AFB, CA	1950-1953	Circle M
97th ARefS, 97th BW	Blytheville AFB, AR	1950-1956	Triangle O
301st ARefS, 301st BW	Lockbourne AFB, OH	1949-1953	Square A
307th ARefS, 307th BW	MacDill AFB, FL/	1953	-
	Kadena AB, Okinawa	1953-1955	-
407th ARefS, 407th SFW	Great Falls AFB/	1954-1957	Green fin cap
	Malmstrom AFB, MT		
509th ARefS, 509th BW	Walker AFB, NM	1951-1954	Triangle C

Notes: ARefS - Air Refueling Squadron
      BW   - Bombardment Wing
      SRW - Strategic Reconnaissance Wing
      FEW - Fighter Escort Wing
      SFW - Strategic Fighter Wing

BOOM OPERATION

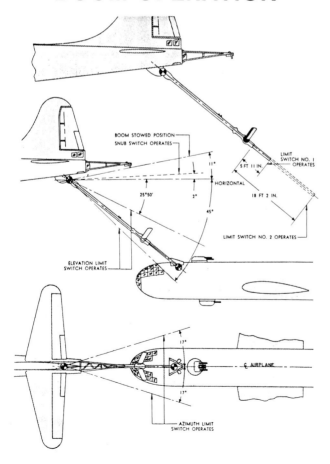

B-29A-10-BN, 42-93921, was converted as the prototype KB-29P tanker. The boom is shown here in the stowed position. The photograph dates from 1949.

(Manion via Williams)

The prototype KB-29P with its boom extended. Stiffeners were added to the aft fuselage between the bomb bay and boom hinge. Refueling indicator lights were mounted on the aft left bomb bay door. Note that the buzz number, BF-921, appears both on the waist and under the left wing. *(Manion via Williams)*

Coverage of the KB-29P continues on page 41.

COLOR GALLERY

Bockscar, B-29-35-MO, 44-27279, as she appeared after restoration at Wright-Patterson AAFld, Ohio.
(Sommerich via Bowers)

*The nose of **Bockscar** as it appeared during World War II. The aircraft shows a tally of having dropped four fat man shapes and the one bomb on Nagasaki.* (Olivi)

*Close-up of the nose art on **Bockscar,** as displayed at Wright-Patterson Air Force Base in the Air Force Museum.* (Kinzey)

Dave's Dream, B-29-40-MO, 44-27354, dropped the first bomb during Operation Crossroads. A 58th Bomb Wing insignia was applied to the forward fuselage. The square B on the tail was for the attack aircraft, as were the black and yellow bands around the aft fuselage and wings. *(USAF KKE576)*

Left: B-29A-40-BN, 44-61669, had been assigned to the 581st ARS&CW. It now carries the markings of the **Mission Inn,** 22nd Bomb Group from March AFB, California, and Korea. The aircraft is now located at the March AFB Museum. *(Lloyd)*

Below: B-29A-50-BN, 44-61825, was flown by LTC Benjamin C. Martin between 1952 and 1956. This ship was assigned to B Flight (blue trim), 582nd Air Resupply and Communications Squadron. This unit was stationed at Molesworth, England. *(Fairbanks)*

The sole YKB-29T, 45-21734, flew with the 421st ARefS. *(Uppstrom)*

The title of Patty Page's song, "Cross Over the Bridge" appeared on the right side of the nose of the YKB-29T. This photograph dates from 1954. *(Uppstrom)*

Lucifer, B-29-97-BW, 45-21746, was one of three Tarzon bomb carriers operated by the 19th Bomb Group during the Korean Conflict. The green nose band indicates the 28th Bomb Squadron. *(Friedrich)*

The left side of *Lucifer's* nose reveals her score - 6 Razon bombs, 10 Tarzon bombs, 2 kills, and 3 purple hearts. *(Friedrich)*

KB-29-55-MO, 44-86418, with a natural metal propeller on the No. 2 engine. (USAF)

The right side of 44-86418. This aircraft operated with the 421st ARefS. (USAF)

This view of 44-86418 reveals the refueling basket tucked into the aft fuselage. (USAF)

KB-29M-90-BW, 44-87742, 43rd ARefS, came to K-2 in Korea to test refueling with the F-84s stationed there in 1951.
(Lippincott via Thompson)

Center left: The prototype boom tanker, KB-29P-10-BN, 42-93921, is shown making a dry hookup with B-29A-65-BN, 44-62205, formerly with the 43rd BG.
(Boeing K1206)

Center right: Here the prototype KB-29P hooks up with EB-29A-65-BN, 44-62205. The white paint was applied to show the flow of spilled fuel. Colored water was used in these tests.
(Boeing K1231)

Left: KB-29P-65-BN, 44-69176, of the 420th Air Refueling Squadron, assigned to the 49th Air Division, USAFE at RFA Sculthorpe, supported fighter-bombers from October 1955 until being replaced by KB-50s in early 1960.
(Brewer)

PACUSAN Dreamboat, *TB-29B-60-BA, 44-84061, was subsequently designated as a YB-29J, with the retrofit of the "Andy Gump" cowlings. The aircraft was photographed at Renton Airport, Washington, prior to its record-setting flight.*
(Boeing K604)

The **PACUSAN Dreamboat** *underwent testing in the Seattle area.*
(Boeing K606)

WB-29A-70-BN, 44-62225, served with the 373rd RS (VLR) Weather in 1948 and the 375th RS (VLR) Weather in 1949. This ship had arctic red trim and carried the MATS insignia on the aft fuselage. A "bug catcher" used for nuclear sampling was carried on the aft fuselage. (USAF KKE 7055)

These WB-29s were assigned to the 72nd Strategic Reconnaissance Squadron (H) at Ladd Field, Alaska, in 1947-1948. They had the arctic red trim and a "bug catcher" in place of the upper aft turret. (Millikan via Thompson)

B-29B-50-BA, was operated by the USAF Flight Test Center at Edwards AFB, California. As indicated by the absence of the bomb bay doors, this aircraft was used as a mother ship. (Bowers)

39

TB-29-75-BW, 44-70039, was one of two such aircraft assigned to the 5015th Radar Evaluation Flight supporting the Alaskan Air Command. Although the turrets were retained, the guns were removed. A radome appears in place of the aft lower turret. *(Fox via Filer)*

VB-29-90-BW, 44-87755, was assigned to the 3rd Air Division, SAC, between August 1954 and December 1955. All armament had been removed. A SAC Milky Way band was applied to the waist. Blue trim was carried on the fin cap and nose gear doors. A hose and drogue refueling fairing appears to be mounted aft of the tail skid. *(via Menard)*

KB-29P Continued

Production KB-29 conversions carried stiffeners along the bomb bay door. Here Air Force personnel discuss the indicator light system. *(Boeing P12858)*

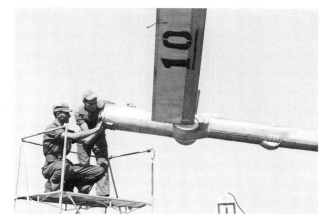

Maintenance technicians inspect a refueling nozzle on a KB-29P being readied for "Fox Peter Two". Tactical numbers were applied to the boom ruddevators, and static discharger wicks were installed on them. *(Boeing P12831)*

The crew of KB-29P-60-BW, 44-69761, awaits the "Fox Peter Two" mission. The last three digits of the serial number were also applied to the forward edge of the forward bomb bay door. These aircraft were equipped with Curtiss electric propellers. *(Boeing P12807)*

Tankers from the 93rd ARefS also supported the "Fox Peter Two" deployment. Here KB-29P-50-BA, 44-84038, and KB-29P-55-BW, 44-69674, undergo checkout. A refueling light was installed at the end of the fixed portion of this boom. *(Boeing P12853)*

A crewman removes the canvas boot from the boom of KB-29P-60-BA, 44-84071, of the 509th ARefS. The 509th ARefS, 509th BW, was assigned to the 8th AF at the time, as denoted by the 8th AF insignia on the dorsal fin fillet. These aircraft were equipped with homing antennas as indicated by the large black fairing on the aft upper fuselage. *(Boeing P12881)*

The boom operator was located in the former tail gunner's compartment. A standard B-29 waist scanner's blister was installed in the tail. *(Boeing P12812)*

KB-29P-45-BA, 44-83943, of the 91st ARefS reveals its unit markings and alignment stripes. One alignment stripe ran lengthwise while ten were crosswise on the belly. The stripes were black. (USAF)

This KB-29P was assigned to the 97th ARefS, 97th BW, as denoted by the Triangle O on the tail. Boots were applied to the cockpit glazing during winter operations. Pennants hang from the bungee cord for the boom boot. (Schultz)

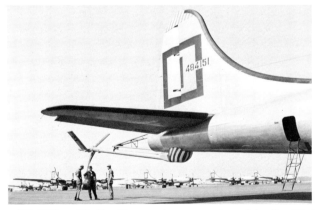

KB-29Ps with the Square I were assigned to the 91st ARefS. The squadron colors appeared on the fin cap, boom hinge fairing, nose gear doors, and waist band. These colors were light blue and white.

(Boeing P12832)

KB-29P-35-BA, 44-83906, with the pilot, Maj. P.M. Karlo-witz, displays the 91st ARefS insignia on the nose.

(Boeing P12809)

YKB-29T

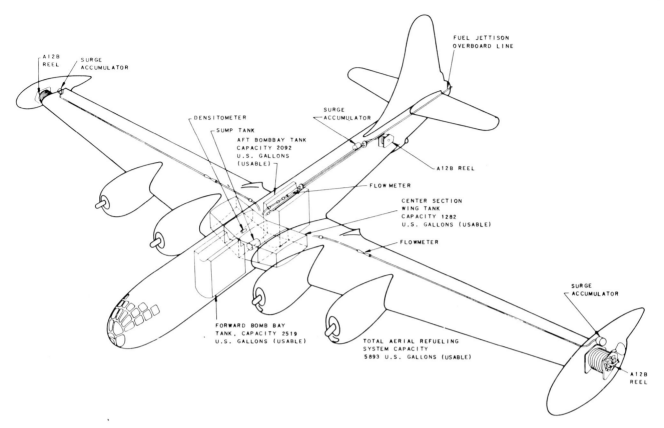

One KB-29M, 45-21734, was converted by the Hayes Aircraft Corporation into the sole YKB-29T equipped with a three-point probe and drogue refueling system. A single reel, replete with fairing, was installed in the aft unpressurized fuselage compartment, while a pair of identical reels was installed in large wingtip fairings. For center of gravity reasons, 600 pounds of ballast had to be added to the tail compartment of the airplane. The fuel supply for refueling was carried in a pair of bomb bay tanks and the wing center section tank, totaling 5,893 gallons being available for transfer. A single-point ground refueling receptacle was installed. The aircraft

was provisioned for a pair of refueling operators located in the aft pressurized compartment at the scanner stations. The right refueling operator controlled the right wing reel unit and the fuselage reel unit, while the left operator controlled the left wing reel unit and the aerial refueling lighting. The radar operator was also located in the aft pressurized compartment.

Electrical system changes included the addition of two DC generators, over-voltage protection, and a greater capacity DC distribution system. Larger capacity AC inverters were installed, these having an automatic changeover feature. The auxiliary power plant was relocated to the tail compartment. A fire detection system and a fire extinguishing system were added. New electronic equipment, external floodlights, rendezvous lights, and taxi lights were installed.

Equipped with R-3350-83 engines and Hamilton Standard hydromatic, non-reversible propellers with electrical de-icing, the airplane was capable of attaining speeds up to 250mph indicated airspeed and cruise at 30,000 feet.

In essence the YKB-29T served as a testbed for the three-point refueling system employed on the KB-50s. The speed of the B-29 did not lend itself well to refueling higher speed jet fighters. It is interesting to note that this aircraft went on to serve operationally with the 421st Air Refueling Squadron, which was known as the "Rainbow Squadron". While in service with this unit, the airplane had a black belly, carried the unit insignia on the left side of the nose and the name **Cross Over the Bridge** after the song performed by Patty Page.

The wingtip hose and drogue pod was tested on the YKB-29T prior to installation on the KB-50s.

(USAF Museum)

AIR RESUPPLY & COMMUNICATIONS

The 580th's inspection dock and hardstands at Wheelus Field, Lybia, as they appeared in 1955. The ramp was shared by B-29s, C-119s, and an SA-16. *(Bernhardt)*

During World War II, special operations were conducted, usually by bombardment groups and squadrons, at night, in bad weather, and in single-ship sorties. Their mission was psychological warfare to include dropping leaflets and/or agents, and they were known as the "Carpetbaggers". Their mission was revived in 1951 with the establishment of the air resupply and communications wings. Officially they were tasked with psychological warfare and unconventional operations. They were activated at Mountain Home AFB, Idaho. A summary of these wings follows:

Wing	Dates	Overseas Base
● 580th AR&CW	4/16/51-9/8/53	Wheelus Field, Lybia
● 581st AR&CW	7/23/51-9/8/53	Clark AB, Philippines
● 582nd AR&CW	9/24/52-10/14/53	Molesworth, England

The wings were downgraded to groups and continued to operate until October 1956. The 581st relocated from Clark Field to Guam during this time.

These units operated a variety of aircraft including: B-29, C-119, SA-16, C-47, C-54, C-118, and H-19.

The B-29s were stripped of all armament. The aft bottom turret was modified to incorporate a sheet metal tub and hatch. An agent would sit on the edge of the tub and await a tap from one of the aircraft scanners. The scanner received his signal over the interphone from the navigator. At 500 feet and in the dark, the agent departed and was never heard from again. He was left to perform his mission. Personnel extraction would be performed by the SA-16s or H-19s.

The aircraft were devoid of markings except for the normal national insignia. The nose gear doors, and occasionally the engine cowl lips, were painted for the flight - red for A flight and blue for B flight. The last three digits of the tail number were usually carried on the nose gear doors.

Because of the nature of their mission, the crews were retained as an integral unit. In addition, they always flew the same aircraft. Because of the idiosyncrasies of individual aircraft, the crews had to be familiar with every nuance of an airplane's performance.

Today the mission of these units is performed by the special operations squadrons assigned to the 23rd Air Force, Military Airlift Command.

B-29-85-BW, 44-87659, assigned to the 580th ARS&CW at Wheelus Field. The nose gear doors were blue, and carried the last three digits of the tail number and the letter B, indicating the B flight. This picture dates from 1954.

(Bernhardt)

B-29A-65-BN, 44-62204, of the 581st ARS&CW at Mountain Home in 1952.　(Bernhardt)

B-29A-50-BN, 44-61884, in the inspection dock at Wheelus Field in 1954.　(Bernhardt)

View of the aft pressurized compartment, looking forward into the bomb bay.　(Bernhardt)

In this view, the agent drop hole may be seen. An access ladder hangs from the aft entry door.　(Fairbanks)

45

F-13/RB-29 RECON VERSIONS

This RB-29A-100-BW, 45-21846, was assigned to the 90th SRW. (Bowers)

Demands for strategic reconnaissance in the Pacific area have always required high-altitude, long-range aircraft because of the nature of the geography. While missions using the same aircraft as those in the European Theater during World War II were initially effective, the loss of allied air bases in southern China during the latter part of 1944 had a serious impact on mapping and reconnaissance in the theater. Aircraft such as the F-5 and F-7, reconnaissance variants of the P-38 Lightning and B-24 Liberator, respectively, were unsatisfactory for the mission. The urgent requirement for an airplane in the theater resulted in the F-13 version of the B-29. It should be noted that between the years of 1930 and 1947, F was the designation carried by photo-reconnaissance aircraft. An initial batch of six F-13s were provided to the XX Bomber Command in the China-Burma-India Theater in August 1944. The tactical availability figures indicate that a total of sixty-one F-13s were available by March 31, 1945. These aircraft were assigned to VLR Reconnaissance Squadrons.

In April 1943, the Aerial Mapping Committee believed that the B-29 was the only airplane in experimental status for which production was planned that would meet all reconnaissance requirements except altitude. However, due to the size of the aircraft, it was not considered to be especially suitable or economical to warrant conversion at that time. By March 1944, the Development Engineering Branch directed the Materiel Command to begin an engineering feasibility study. A month later, a VLR reconnaissance project was established with an initial allocation of twelve B-29s for the program. Some delays were encountered. One reason was that a camera designed for use with the AN/APQ-13 radar was not readily available. A decision to incorporate all standard aircraft modifications on the prototype F-13 resulted in additional delays. The first test flight took place on August 4, 1944, at the Continental-Denver Modification Center.

The Air Service Technical Command in concert with the Boeing Airplane Company, prime airframe manufacturer, and the Fairchild Camera and Instrument Company, developed the photo-reconnaissance version of the B-29. The F-13A crew complement would consist of the full eleven-man combat crew plus a photographer and a cameraman. A battery of six cameras were installed on the aircraft.

For photomapping an area 20-30 miles (varying with altitude), three K-17 cameras in a trimetrogon mount were employed. The A-5 film magazine with a 150-foot roll of film was used to take 9x9 inch photographs, while the A-9 contained 390-feet of film. Fairchild manufactured the A-5 while the Mills Novelty Company produced the A-9.

For highly detailed photo interpretation and reconnaissance work, a pair of K-22 cameras were carried in a split vertical mount. At 20,000 feet, these cameras were capable of photographing a strip about two miles wide. Either an A-5 or A-9 film magazine could be employed with the K-22.

A K-18 camera mounted vertically covered a wider range than the K-22s and had a larger negative. An A-8 film magazine with 390 feet of film was used with the K-18 camera. The exposed film was 9x18 inches. The A-8 magazine was manufactured by the Payne Furnace Company, Hunter and Company, and Fairchild. In addition, a K-19 camera could be carried for night photography. Fairchild manufactured the K-17, K-18, and K-19, and K-22 cameras. Also, the Folmer Graflex Corporation produced the K-17.

Because of the altitude flown by the F-13, and the fact that the cameras were carried within the pressurized cabin, special glass was employed in the camera windows. These ¾-inch-thick plate glass windows were manufactured by the Pittsburgh Plate Glass Company. The Robinson Aviation Company built the camera mounts, while the intervalometer was made by the Central Scientific Company.

A special sight was installed in the nose for the photo-navigator. This sight was adapted from the B-3 driftmeter. A control panel for the photo-navigator was installed in the nose of the airplane. All cameras and the camera operator's station were located in the aft pressurized compartment. After 1947 the reconnaissance Superfortresses were redesignated RB-29s.

Double Exposure, F-13A-5-BN, 42-93855, was assigned to C Flight, 1st PRS, Hq & Hq Squadron, XX Bomber Command, in the China-Burma-India Theater. The unit was activated at Hsinching, the forward operating base of the 40th BG in China. Colors on the nose art are: medium blue hat, blond hair, red bathing suit, white shoes, and name in red with blue shadow. (Morrison)

Poison Ivy, F-13A, 42-24585, of the 3rd PRS.   (USAF)

*This **Double Exposure**, F-13A-55-BW, 42-24877, operated with the 3rd PRS, XXI Bomber Command, from Saipan. She was flown by 1/Lt. Thomas C. Kendall.*
(USAF)

The other side of 42-24877 after she bellied in at night on Saipan.   (via Morrison)

Quan Yin Cha Ara, F-13A-5-BN, 42-93853, originally served in the CBI with the 1st PRS as one of the four original ships in the unit. She later went on to serve with the 3rd PRS on Saipan. The F was applied to the nose and tail after arrival in the Marianas.   (Patterson)

*The other side of **Quan Yin Cha Ara,** with three kills and fifteen missions to her credit. The nose was toned down after the arrival of the nurses on Saipan.   (Patterson)*

Drift sight and camera controls located in the photo-navigator's (ex-bombardier) station.   (USAF Museum)

Radio operator's position, looking forward.

(USAF Museum)

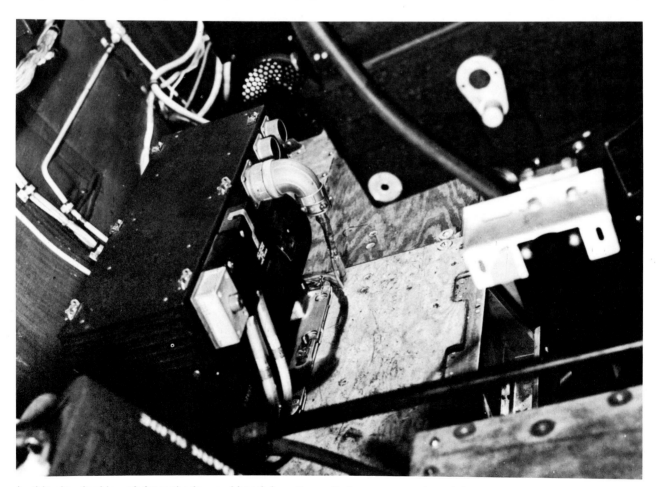

In this view looking aft from the forward bomb bay, the radio frequency and modulator units may be seen above the antenna fairing for the AN/APQ-13 radar.

(USAF Museum)

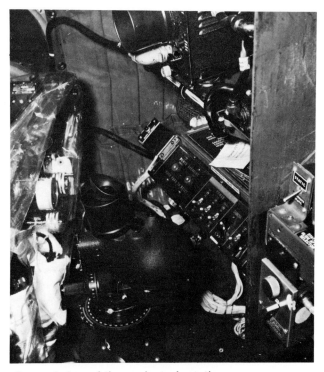

General view of the navigator's station.

(USAF Museum)

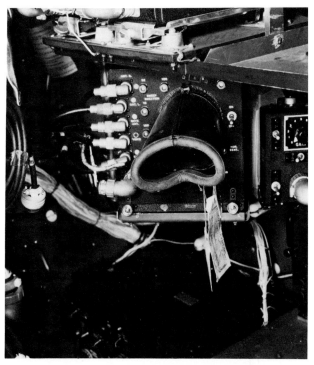

View looking forward at the navigator's station.

(USAF Museum)

View looking forward from the aft cabin access door for the PU-7/AP inverters.

(USAF Museum)

Camera compartment instrument panel with a B-3A intervalometer for each group of cameras. (NASM)

Photo-navigator's station in the nose of the airplane. (NASM)

Vertical camera installation. (NASM)

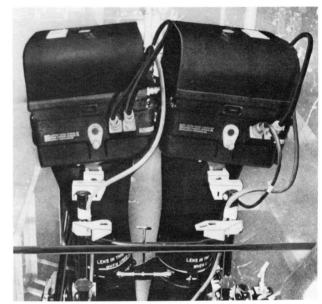

Split vertical camera installation. (NASM)

View looking aft at left trimetrogon camera installation. (NASM)

View looking aft at vertical camera and the split vertical cameras. (NASM)

F·13 PHOTOGRAPHIC AIRPLANE (B-29)

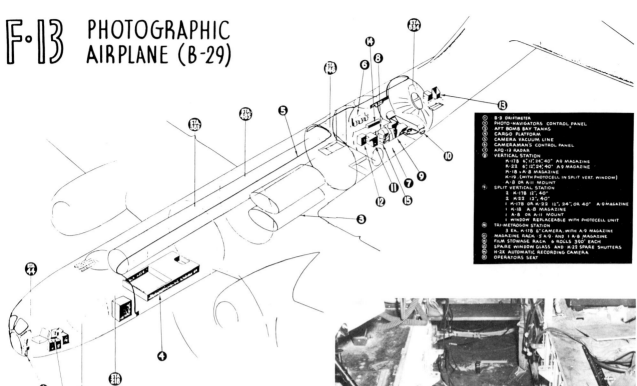

① B-3 DRIFTMETER
② PHOTO-NAVIGATOR'S CONTROL PANEL
③ AFT BOMB BAY TANKS
④ CARGO PLATFORM
⑤ CAMERA VACUUM LINE
⑥ CAMERAMAN'S CONTROL PANEL
⑦ APQ-13 RADAR
⑧ VERTICAL STATION
  K-17B 6", 12", 24", 40" A9 MAGAZINE
  K-22 6", 12", 24", 40" A9 MAGAZINE
  K-18 + A-8 MAGAZINE
  K-19 (WITH PHOTOCELL IN SPLIT VERT. WINDOW)
  A-8 OR A-11 MOUNT
⑨ SPLIT VERTICAL STATION
  2 K-17B 12", 40"
  2 K-22 12", 40"
  1 K-17B OR K-22 12", 24", OR 40" A-9 MAGAZINE
  1 K-18 A-8 MAGAZINE
  1 A-8 OR A-11 MOUNT
  1 WINDOW REPLACEABLE WITH PHOTOCELL UNIT
⑩ TRI-METROGON STATION
  3 EA. K-17B 6" CAMERA, WITH A-9 MAGAZINE
⑪ MAGAZINE RACK · 5 A-9 · AND 1 A-8 MAGAZINE
⑫ FILM STOWAGE RACK · 6 ROLLS 390' EACH
⑬ SPARE WINDOW GLASS AND K-22 SPARE SHUTTERS
⑭ K-2X AUTOMATIC RECORDING CAMERA
⑮ OPERATORS SEAT

Interior view of the camera well looking forward.
(USAF Museum)

Camera windows were cut into the bottom of the aft
pressurized compartment.   (USAF Museum)

Camera window in the left side of the aft pressurized
compartment.   (USAF Museum)

Interior view of the camera well looking aft.
(USAF Museum)

SB-29

SB-29-60-BA, 44-84078, operated with the 3rd ARSq during the Korean Conflict.   *(USAF 79592USAF)*

A total of sixteen B-29s were modified for the search and rescue mission and served with the Air Rescue Service within the Military Air Transport Service. Modifications to the airplane consisted of relocating the AN/APQ-13 radome from between the bomb bay doors to the forward lower turret position. The radio operator's position was moved from behind the forward turret to the waist compartment. A crew of eleven was carried: two pilots, a navigator, two flight engineers, two radio operators, a radar operator, and three scanners, two in the waist and one in the tail.

The most notable change to the airplane was the installation of the A-3 airborne lifeboat manufactured by the Edo Corporation, College Point, Long Island, New York. The aluminum alloy hull, built in aircraft-type construction, had a hull measuring 29 feet 9 inches. The boat had twenty watertight compartments and two rubberized fabric self-righting chambers, one at the bow and the other at the stern. The self-righting chambers were automatically inflated when the boat was released from the airplane. The cockpit was self-draining. Power was provided by an inboard engine driving a single screw. The boat had a range of 500 miles.

The A-3 lifeboat was carried externally, stern-first. Both mechanical and pneumatic release mechanisms were incorporated into the B-29, with the controls located in the bombardier's station. A displacing linkage would guide the boat away from the airplane. The boat dropped at a fifty degree bow-down attitude, and was suspended by a single 100 foot diameter parachute. Fins attached to the bow of the boat stabilized the descent. These fins could be discarded by the boat occupants. For ground handling, the boat had a three-point beaching gear installed. While the two main wheels supported the weight, the bow wheel was used for steering the boat under the airplane. Jackscrews in the beaching gear permitted raising the boat up to the airplane. The beaching gear was removed prior to flight.

The B-29 inventory for Air Rescue Service was as follows:

1947-1949	3	1952	19
1950	7	1953	16
1951	9	1954	17
		1955	14

Three B-29s in ARS were never modified to carry the A-3 lifeboat. The following airplanes were converted into SB-29s:

B-29A-40-BN	44-61671	B-29-60-BA	44-84088
B-29-70-BW	44-69957	B-29-60-BA	44-84098
B-29-70-BW	44-69971	B-29-65-BA	44-84112
B-29-80-BW	44-70119	B-29-45-MO	44-86303
B-29-55-BA	44-84030	B-29-45-MO	44-86308
B-29-60-BA	44-84078	B-29-85-BW	44-87644
B-29-60-BA	44-84084	B-29-85-BW	44-87665
B-29-60-BA	44-84086	B-29-90-BW	44-87761

On February 24, 1951, an SB-29 assigned to Flight D, 11th AR Squadron, dropped an A-3 lifeboat to twelve survivors of the SS Florentine, which had sunk in the western Pacific.

During July 1951, SA-16s and SB-29s from the 4th and 5th AR Squadrons dropped supplies to flood victims in Kansas and Missouri. An A-3 lifeboat was dropped and was credited with saving 439 persons in one day of the rescue effort.

An RB-36 declared an emergency over the North Atlantic on August 5, 1953. Two engines were on fire and the crew ditched south of Ireland. Both the 67th and 68th AR Squadrons responded. The wreckage was located and an A-3 lifeboat was dropped to the four survivors. Surface vessels were directed for the pick up.

On September 5, 1953, the 3rd AR Group dispatched two SB-29s and four SA-16s to assist the survivors of a U.S. Navy P2V Neptune which was shot down in the Sea

SB-29-80-BW, 44-70119, had an additional search radar installed in the aft top turret location. The proximity of the stern of the A-3 lifeboat to the AN/APQ-13 radome may be seen in this view. (Boeing 139629)

of Japan by Russian fighters. Nine survivors were picked up by an SA-16 and flown to Misawa AB, Japan.

During the Korean Conflict, the 2nd and 3rd AR Squadrons had responsibility for supporting the combat aircraft in the Far East Air Forces. The 2nd ARSq provided SB-29s to follow the FEAF B-29s to the penetration point along the Korean coast. The SB-29s would orbit until the bombers returned. The 2nd ARSq was stationed in the Philippines and Okinawa. The 3rd ARSq was head-quartered at Johnson AB, Japan, and had detachments at Yokota, Misawa, and Ashyia. The inventory of the 3rd ARSq included SB-29s, SB-17s, SC-47s, SA-16s, and

L-5s. The maximum strength of SB-29s employed during the Korean Conflict was four. When the B-29s began night operations, underwing flare pods were installed on the SB-29s to enhance their night rescue capabilities. Fortunately no night rescue had to be made, but the morale of the bomber crews was boosted.

SB-29-70-BW, 44-69971, escorts a fellow B-29 with its number four engine feathered. In many instances the SB-29 would provide escort only and not have to drop its boat. (USAF)

B-29A-40-BN, 44-61671, was the first B-29 converted for rescue work. (via Williams)

The first SB-29 is shown releasing the A-3 lifeboat. The release mechanism may be seen under the fuselage. The old buzz number, BF-671, appears on the waist. (USAF via Boeing)

SB-29-60-BA, 44-84088, operated with Flight D, 11th ARSq, out of Andersen AFB, Guam. The flare pod, installed for night operations, was located under the wing. The mast antennas under the wing are for the radio altimeter. (USAF via Boeing)

Interior details of the Edo lifeboat. The engine controls were located in the box adjacent to the wheel on the left. (Edo)

Ordnance personnel load a flare in the right wing pod of a Flight D, 11th ARSq SB-29. (USAF via Williams)

The Edo lifeboat with its foul weather cover removed. (Edo)

The Edo A-3 airborne lifeboat is shown here with its beaching gear and foul weather cover. (Edo)

WB-29

WB-29A-70-BN, 44-62214, was assigned to the 58th RS (M) Weather, at Eielson AFB, Alaska, in 1951. This aircraft was devoid of markings except for the arctic red trim. Dual ADF radio loop antennas were installed on top of the airplane.
(USAF)

Weather reconnaissance WB-29s were derived through modification of standard bombardment B-29s. All armament and associated equipment was removed, and the remaining holes were faired over. An astrodome was installed in the forward upper turret location. A crew of ten was comprised of: two pilots, flight engineer, weather observer, navigator (in the forward compartment) and radio operator, left scanner (dropsonde operator), radiosonde operator, and right scanner (crew chief). For some missions, an additional weather observer was carried in the tail compartment. Numerous items of radio equipment were carried as listed in the table on page 62.

Specialized meteorological equipment installed on the airplanes consisted of:

- ML-313/AM Psychrometer - A pair of thermometers (one wet and one dry) used to measure the water vapor content of the atmosphere.
- ID/AMQ-2 Aerograph - A relative humidity indicator.
- SCR-718 Radio Altimeter
- AN/APN-1 Radar Altimeter
- AN/AMT-3 Radiosonde Unit - Parachute dropped units transmitted temperature, humidity, and pressure data back to the airplane.

On occasion the Air Weather Service (AWS) was requested to fly nuclear sampling missions. For these operations, the airplanes were equipped with air filter assemblies nicknamed "bug catchers". These units were mounted in the aft upper turret location.

AWS obtained their B-29s in 1946, with their primary mission being weather reconnaissance. However, on November 23, 1946, the AAF assigned the weather reconnaissance squadrons a secondary mission of bombardment within the capabilities of the B/RB-29s assigned. The AAF reasoned that they wanted to maintain a latent combat capability in these crews should this role become necessary. B-29s initially assigned to the AWS carried the full complement of armament. By 1950,

most of these airplanes had been modified to the WB-29 configuration and the armament had been removed. However, shortly after the outbreak of the Korean Conflict, the defensive armament was replaced. The tail guns were readily installed, while the central fire control system (CFC) and remote turrets were added only to the airplanes within the combat zone. While never training for the bombardment role, the 514th RS, based at Guam, actually participated in a practice bombing run against Tokyo on July 5, 1948, and dropped 500-pound bombs on a practice range on Medinilla Island north of Guam. By July 15th, AWS was relieved of this role.

The AWS gained the 53rd, 54th, 55th, and 59th Reconnaissance Squadrons VLR (Weather) on March 13, 1946, when they were reassigned from the Continental Air Command's 311th Reconnaissance Wing. (The 113th RW would soon be assigned to the newly formed Strategic Air Command). The 308th Reconnaissance Group (Weather) was activated at Morrison Field, Florida, on October 17, 1946, and assigned to the Air Weather Service, Military Air Transport Service. The 308th RG gained the 53rd Reconnaissance Squadron VLR (Weather), stationed at Grenier Field, New Hampshire, and the 59th Reconnaissance Squadron VLR (Weather), stationed at Castle Field, California. The 53rd RS had lineage to the 3rd Weather Reconnaissance Squadron which had seen wartime service over the North Atlantic. On November 8, 1946, the 53rd relocated to Morrison Field, Florida. The 59th RS, activated at Will Rogers Field, Oklahoma, on August 10, 1945, and after several changes arrived at Castle Field, California, on January 26, 1946. The mission of the 308th RG and its two component squadrons, the 53rd and 59th, was to train in the B-29 Superfortress. Subsequently, the 54th and 55th RSs were added to the 308th for training. These latter squadrons were stationed at Morrison Field, Florida, from October 17, 1946. On June 11, 1947, the 54th RS was assigned to North Field, Guam. The 55th RS was relocated to Fairfield-Suisun

B-29-90-BW, 45-21717, belonged to the 308th Weather Group based at Fairfield-Suisun when this photograph was taken in September 1948. This ship was equipped with Curtiss electric propellers. The standard MATS colors were applied to the fin band - blue with yellow edges and the lettering in white. An Air Weather Service insignia was applied to the fin fillet. **WEATHER RECONNAISSANCE** *appeared in white on the black belly above the nose gear door. The standard MATS wing on the forward fuselage was reversed - blue with yellow edges. The unit identifier appeared in the circle.*

(Larkins)

Army Air Field, California, on July 1, 1947. On October 15, 1947, both the 54th and 55th RSs were inactivated and became the 514th and 374th RSs, respectively. The 53rd RS moved from Grenier Field to Kindley Field, Bermuda, on July 1, 1947, was inactivated on October 15, 1947, and redesignated the 373rd RS. The 59th RS left Fairfield-Suisun for Ladd Field, Alaska, on May 7, 1947, and was inactivated on October 15, 1947. It was reactivated as the 375th RS the following day.

The 512th RS VLR (W) was activated at Gravelly Point, Virginia, on October 15, 1947, and was equipped with B-29s. The 512th was assigned to the 308th RG. Between September 20, 1948, and February 13, 1949, the 512th was in limbo, and then stationed at Fairfield-Suisun AFB and equipped with RB-29s. The 512th was reassigned to the 2143rd Air Weather Wing on February 13, 1949. The squadron deployed to Yokota Air Base, Japan, arriving on January 27, 1950. Within twenty-four hours of the outbreak of the Korean Conflict, the 512th flew an RB-29 on a weather reconnaissance mission over the battle area.

The 56th Strategic Reconnaissance Squadron VLR (Weather) was activated at Misawa Air Base, Japan, on February 21, 1951. The RB/WB-29s of the 56th and 512th flew combat weather reconnaissance missions north of the 38th Parallel every day until June 9, 1952. These were the only USAF units to make such a claim during the war. Because of enemy flak and fighters encountered on some of their earliest missions, a request was made for the AWS to reinstall the tail armament on their B-29s. A total of ten of the 512th's RB/WB-29s had the .50 caliber guns installed by September 1950, and the remaining two airplanes were so equipped shortly thereafter. No other AWS WB-29 squadron was so armed, and these guns were removed once the airplanes were no longer required to fly over hostile areas in Korea.

Initial flights during the Korean Conflict were flown like normal weather reconnaissance missions. However, shipping surveillance, visual reconnaissance, and ECM

reconnaissance within their capabilities was added. Initially these flights were flown at 10,000 feet over the Sea of Japan approximately 100 miles off the Korean coast, and to within 100 miles of Vladivostok. By early July 1950, the 512th RS was flying two fixed tracks per day over or near enemy territory, and began dropping leaflets from 18,000 feet over southwestern Korea. In the beginning these leaflets were dropped from the rear entrance door and the nose wheel well door. These drops were made after depressurizing the airplane. Subsequently, the drops were made from the bomb bay, making it unnecessary to depressurize.

On July 13, 1950, and on two other occasions, 1/Lt Fred R. Spies piloted a 512th RS RB-29 with Major General Emmett "Rosie" O'Donnell, FEAF Commander, on board. The airplane led the first B-29 strike from Japan against North Korea installations. This airplane served as an airborne command post and weather station, giving on-the-spot weather reports and directions to the inbound bombers. For the July 13th mission, and two other missions, Lt Spies was awarded his first oak leaf cluster for his Distinguished Flying Cross.

The first weather reconnaissance missions in Korea were named "Buzzard Special." By early September 1950, a fixed synoptic track over North Korea was established and was named "Buzzard King". In July 1952, the name was changed to "Buzzard Kilo". This track called for the RB-29s to fly up the Yellow Sea, eastward across Korea, and south to Japan over the Sea of Japan. The flights were timed so that they would arrive at the western coast of Korea by sunset and make their crossing of hostile territory at night. Rarely was fighter escort available. These flights were over hostile territory, thus making the crews eligible for the Air Medal. In accordance with international agreements, their data transmissions were made uncoded in the clear. While such data was available from Russia, none was broadcast from China or North Korea. For this reason, it is believed that the WB-29s were trailed, but never downed. By mid-1952, the

AWS directives were changed relative to hostile territory overflights and the synoptic track was moved south of the 38th Parallel. Just forty-eight hours after the track was moved south, FEAF Bomber Command lost three B-29s in the Pyongyang area to enemy night fighters. From June 1952, until the end of the Korean Conflict, the AWS B-29s never again ventured north of the 38th Parallel.

During "Operation Vittles," the Berlin Airlift, the 374th RS provided four WB-29s and crews for coordinated operations with the 18th Weather Squadron at Wiesbaden, West Germany, and 3rd Air Division at Bushy Park, London. "Lark Easy" was the first synoptic track, a 2,080-nautical mile, eleven-hour track over the Atlantic southwest of England. On December 8, 1948, the first "Lark Easy" mission was flown. After two weeks, a new track "Lark George" was established. This was an 843-nautical mile, seven-hour daylight track which was first flown on December 30th.

The first low-level night penetration of a hurricane was flown by RB-29, 45-21819, assigned to the 373rd RS. This mission was flown on October 19, 1949, during Hurricane Love, while it was some 340 nautical miles south-southeast of Bermuda.

In October 1954, Edward R. Murrow and a television crew from his show "See It Now" flew aboard WB-29, 44-69987, **Hurricane Hunters,** of the 53rd WRS. Following the flight, Murrow was reported to have said, "The eye of a hurricane is an excellent place to reflect upon the puniness of man and his works. If an adequate definition of humility is ever written, it's likely to be done in the eye of a hurricane." They had penetrated Hurricane Edna.

On October 7, 1946, a B-29, piloted by Major Paul E. Fackler, became the first to fly near the top of a hurricane. They departed Morrison Field, Florida, at 12:32 Eastern Standard Time, with surface winds of twenty-eight mph. A spiraling climb was made to 20,000 feet, where they encountered winds of seventy mph. A general heading toward the storm center, some 350 miles to the southwest, was assumed. The crew went on instruments as they penetrated the northeast wall of the storm. At 31,000 feet they encountered winds in excess of 100 mph which were shifting rapidly. At that altitude the "eye" was not clear as experienced at lower altitudes, however the air was smooth. Unmistakable ring-like clouds appeared on the radar scope within the storm center. For about two and a half hours the airplane probed the storm making five penetrations. The roof of the storm was around 36,000 feet. The estimated winds in the hurricane were in excess of 170 mph, and a maximum altitude of 31,000 feet was achieved during this flight. The flight was to terminate at Patterson Field, Dayton, Ohio, where the data could be analyzed. However, the fuel consumed getting to altitude precluded this destination. Surface winds at Cuba were reported at sixty mph making landing difficult. Consequently, they recovered at Guatamala City, Guatamala, after a grueling eight hour flight.

A Ptarmigan is a far-ranging arctic bird. The 58th Strategic Weather Reconnaissance Squadron named their flights over the North Pole in honor of these birds. The purpose of these flights was to gather meteorological data from the polar region known as the "arctic weather factory." Storms spawned in this area strike Canada and the United States within a few days of their inception. Ptarmigan missions routinely lasted fifteen to sixteen hours. The initial polar flights were based on supposition or vague information gleaned from obscure sources, and crews did not want to fly during the transition periods between day and night for fear of becoming lost. The lighting conditions precluded use of celestial navigation, and radio reception was impossible due to precipitation static. A major breakthrough came with the use of the Pfund Sky Compass, an ingenious device enabling the navigator to take a bearing on the polarized rays of the sun after it has sunk below the horizon. Initially these missions were flown by the 375th Reconnaissance Squadron (VLR) Weather, activated at Ladd Field, Alaska, on October 16, 1947, and moving to Eielson AFB, Alaska, on March 6, 1949. The 375th was inactivated on February 20, 1951. In its place, the 58th Strategic Reconnaissance Squadron, Medium (Weather), was activated on February 21, 1951. Captain Edward N. Pollock piloted the **Lonesome Polecat,** B-29, 44-62151, on the 375th Ptarmigan flight. Rear Admiral Clifton A.F. Sprague, USN, commander of the Alaskan Sea Command, was the honorary commander for the flight. The 500th Ptarmigan flight was made by the 58th SWRS in B-29, 44-62197, with Captain Pat Bass as aircraft commander. The takeoff weight for a B-29 on a Ptarmigan flight was between 130,000-134,000 pounds. Two tons of survival gear was carried, and about 7800 gallons of gasoline were consumed on each mission. During the flights, the outside air temperatures ranged from -30° to -60° F. The flights were conducted using the autopilot in order to maintain the precise headings required by the navigator. However, the autopilot was constantly monitored because of its inherent precess characteristics.

In September 1952, Captain W.E. Beard of the 54th Strategic Weather Reconnaissance Squadron based at Anderson AFB, Guam, piloted a WB-29 from the bottom to the top of a typhoon. The airplane approached the storm at an altitude of 800 feet. The surface winds were 120 mph. Without warning the airplane dropped to 300 feet. An 180-degree turn was out of the question, and the crew worked to maintain a course directly into the base of the foulest, blackest and meanest-looking cloud imaginable. Directional control was difficult to maintain. The airplane was driven from 300 to 6000 feet while being subjected to sever turbulence. The weather techncian became sick and unstrapped himself and suddenly was pinned against the top of the fuselage. The airplane entered the eye of the typhoon and the observer proceeded to make his soundings and collect the data. Because of the severe conditions encountered, the crew

Polar Queen, B-29A-65-BN, 44-62163, was operated by the 59th RS (VLR) Weather, Ladd Field, Alaska. This picture dates from 1947. The barber pole on the nose denote flights to/over the North Pole. The birds were for Ptarmigan flights. *(USAF)*

Lonesome Polecat, B-29A-65-BN, 44-62151, was assigned to the 375th RS (VLR) Weather, at Ladd Field, in 1948. *(USAF)*

Center left: **Duffy's Tavern**, B-29A-70-BN, 44-62216, displays a number of Ptarmigan's on the nose. She was assigned to the 375th RS (VLR) Weather in 1948.

Center right: **Typhoon Goon**, B-29-95-BW, 45-21838, was operated by the 514th RS (VLR) Weather, from North Field, Guam, in 1950. A total of 24 storm eye penetration symbols appeared on the nose. The insignia on the nose was left over from the airplane's previous assignment with the 514th BS, 498th BG. It was a challenge to fly this bird in the weather recee role - there was severe corrosion in the wing center section and rivets popped on every flight. *(USAF)*

Right: **Hurricane Hunters**, WB-29-70-BW, 44-69987, was flown out of Kindley Field, Bermuda, by the 53rd RS (M) Weather. The squadron insignia was applied to the nose. *(USAF)*

departed the storm in such a manner as to experience the least turbulence. They climbed to 13,500 feet to make their departure. A subsequent ground inspection revealed no structural damage. On the following day the aircraft carried emergency supplies to Wake Island.

The 53rd Reconnaissance Squadron (VLR) Weather, operated out of Kindley Field, Bermuda, from August 17, 1947. The unit was inactivated on October 17, 1947, and was reactivated as the 53rd Strategic Reconnaissance Squadron, Medium, Weather, on February 21, 1951. While the U.S. Navy assumed responsibility for weather

reconnaissance in the Caribbean area, the 53rd tracked hurricanes over the west central Atlantic area. On November 7, 1953, the 53rd relocated to Burtonwood, England. On February 15, 1954, the unit was redesignated the 53rd Weather Reconnaissance Squadron. For the Christmas of 1953, the children of the 53rd RS prevailed upon their fathers to take their letters to Santa Claus because they flew over the North Pole. Soon the word spread and letters from all over Britain were carried. These letters were dropped from the WB-29s as they crossed the North Pole. By the Christmas of 1955, letters

This B-29-95-BW was assigned to the 57th RS (M) Weather, based at Hickham AFB, Hawaii, in 1951. Arctic red trim was applied to the outer wing panels and empennage. The reversed MATS trim was applied to the forward fuselage.

(USAF)

from all over Europe were carried to Santa. The 53rd WRS was inactivated on March 18, 1960.

Between 1945 and 1960, the 53rd experienced only two major accidents. On September 18, 1953, a WB-29 was returning to Kindley from Hunter AFB, Georgia, when trouble occurred approximately 150 miles east of Charleston, South Carolina. The No. 3 propeller ran away, departed the engine, hit the No. 4 engine, severing fuel and oil lines, and caused a series of explosions and a fire. The right wing failed and the airplane went into a flat spin. The tail came off and the airplane disintegrated upon impact with the water. Nine survivors were picked up the following day after they spent the night battling the sea and sharks. Seven crewmen were lost.

The second major accident occurred on October 25, 1955, when a WB-29 was around seventy miles from RAF Burtonwood. Trouble began when the airplane was approximately 1200 miles west of the northern tip of Ireland when a fuel boost pump failed. Three hours later, as the airplane neared Prestwick, Scotland, the No. 1 engine failed. The No. 2 and 3 engines quit a few minutes later. The crew bailed out, and in about thirty seconds the plane stalled and fell to the ground. All eleven crewmen made safe landings, although one sergeant landed in a pen with an excited pig.

Initially the AWS B-29s were configured essentially as standard bombardment airplanes. Their primary mission was training. Their actual weather reconnaissance missions consisted of flying into storm areas and making visual observations within the limits of the aircrews and the equipment. Altitude, airspeed, and drift information, coupled with temperature readings and a visual assessment of clouds and precipitation, were the extent of their

capabilities. The 308th RG operated B-29s between October 17, 1946, and June 31, 1949, and TB-29s between September 1, 1948, and February 1, 1949. Headquarters for the 308th RG was Morrison Field, Florida, from October 17, 1946, until June 30, 1947. They moved to Fairfield-Suisun AAFld, California, on July 1, 1947, and remained until November 9, 1949. RB-29s, configured for the weather reconnaissance role, came into the inventory on July 1, 1949, and continued in operation until March 1, 1950. The WB-29s were in the inventory between March 1, 1950, and January 5, 1951. The 308th RG moved to Tinker AFB, Oklahoma, on November 10, 1949, and remained until January 5, 1951. With the introduction of the RB/WB-29s, the air weather mission was greatly expanded. They then had the specialized equipment for performing meaningful weather reconnaissance operations. With the advent of nuclear weapons testing, the AWS B-29s got into full swing. They performed sampling flights before, during, and after every test from 1949 on. It was not unusual for a sampling airplane to leave the blast area covered with "hot" mud, and have the crew search for rain clouds to wash the ship before returning to base. Otherwise, the airplane had to be hosed down before the crew could deplane.

When the weather B-29s were on the ground, they had ground electrical power applied to all radios and instruments to prevent the shock of cold from system cycling. Much as the commercial airlines have learned, a flying airplane is more reliable than one that sits because of deterioration of hydraulic seals and the general disuse of the various airplane systems. The AWS B-29s did much to prove cold weather and polar operations, and developed proficiency in sustained operations under adverse conditions.

Above: The weather observer sat in the former bombardier's station. A weather instrument panel was installed. Here the observer takes readings from the psychrometer. (USAF)

Right: Here a crewman places a dropsonde in its chamber. The pressure gauges appear on the chamber tube. (USAF)

ANTENNA LOCATIONS

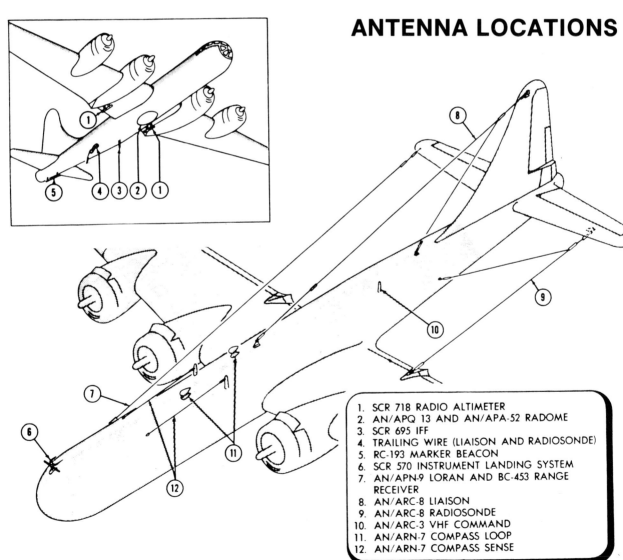

1. SCR 718 RADIO ALTIMETER
2. AN/APQ 13 AND AN/APA-52 RADOME
3. SCR 695 IFF
4. TRAILING WIRE (LIAISON AND RADIOSONDE)
5. RC-193 MARKER BEACON
6. SCR 570 INSTRUMENT LANDING SYSTEM
7. AN/APN-9 LORAN AND BC-453 RANGE RECEIVER
8. AN/ARC-8 LIAISON
9. AN/ARC-8 RADIOSONDE
10. AN/ARC-3 VHF COMMAND
11. AN/ARN-7 COMPASS LOOP
12. AN/ARN-7 COMPASS SENSE

COMMUNICATION EQUIPMENT LOCATIONS

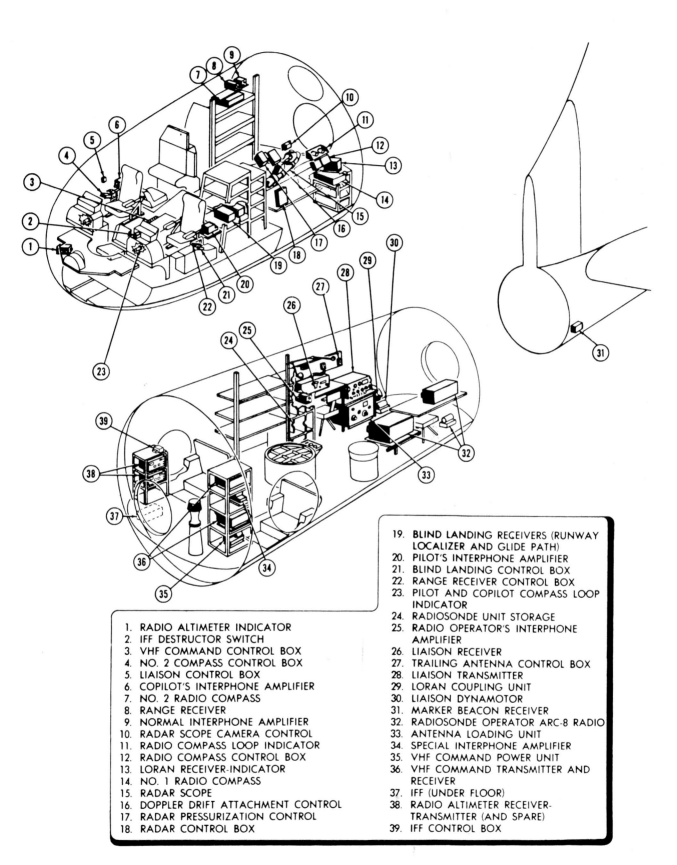

1. RADIO ALTIMETER INDICATOR
2. IFF DESTRUCTOR SWITCH
3. VHF COMMAND CONTROL BOX
4. NO. 2 COMPASS CONTROL BOX
5. LIAISON CONTROL BOX
6. COPILOT'S INTERPHONE AMPLIFIER
7. NO. 2 RADIO COMPASS
8. RANGE RECEIVER
9. NORMAL INTERPHONE AMPLIFIER
10. RADAR SCOPE CAMERA CONTROL
11. RADIO COMPASS LOOP INDICATOR
12. RADIO COMPASS CONTROL BOX
13. LORAN RECEIVER-INDICATOR
14. NO. 1 RADIO COMPASS
15. RADAR SCOPE
16. DOPPLER DRIFT ATTACHMENT CONTROL
17. RADAR PRESSURIZATION CONTROL
18. RADAR CONTROL BOX

19. BLIND LANDING RECEIVERS (RUNWAY LOCALIZER AND GLIDE PATH)
20. PILOT'S INTERPHONE AMPLIFIER
21. BLIND LANDING CONTROL BOX
22. RANGE RECEIVER CONTROL BOX
23. PILOT AND COPILOT COMPASS LOOP INDICATOR
24. RADIOSONDE UNIT STORAGE
25. RADIO OPERATOR'S INTERPHONE AMPLIFIER
26. LIAISON RECEIVER
27. TRAILING ANTENNA CONTROL BOX
28. LIAISON TRANSMITTER
29. LORAN COUPLING UNIT
30. LIAISON DYNAMOTOR
31. MARKER BEACON RECEIVER
32. RADIOSONDE OPERATOR ARC-8 RADIO
33. ANTENNA LOADING UNIT
34. SPECIAL INTERPHONE AMPLIFIER
35. VHF COMMAND POWER UNIT
36. VHF COMMAND TRANSMITTER AND RECEIVER
37. IFF (UNDER FLOOR)
38. RADIO ALTIMETER RECEIVER-TRANSMITTER (AND SPARE)
39. IFF CONTROL BOX

TABLE OF COMMUNICATION AND ASSOCIATED ELECTRONIC EQUIPMENT.

TYPE	DESIGNATION	USE	PRIMARY OPERATOR	RANGE	LOCATIONS OF CONTROLS
1. Interphone	AN/AIC-2 (modified)	Crew intercommunication and use with other radio equipment	All crew members	Crew stations within the aircraft	All crew stations
2. VHF Command	AN/ARC-3	Short range, two-way, voice and code communication	Pilot, Copilot	30 miles at 1000 feet	Pilots' aisle stand
3. Radio Range Receiver	BC-453	Reception of range code and voice signals	Pilot	200 miles	Pilot's control stand
4. Liaison	AN/ARC-8	Long range, two way, voice and code communication	Radio Operator	Up to 5000 miles at high frequency	Radio Operator's table
5. Radiosonde Radio Set	AN/ARC-8	Receives and transmits weather information	Radiosonde Operator	Up to 5000 miles at high frequency	Radiosonde Operator's table
6. Radiosonde	AN/AMT-3	Transmits weather signals automatically when dropped by parachute	Radiosonde Operator		Integral with unit
7. Radio Compass No. 1	AN/ARN-7	Reception of signals for direction bearing, homing, and radio range flying	Navigator	200 miles	Navigator's station
8. Radio Compass No. 2	AN/ARN-7	Reception of signals for direction bearing, homing, and radio range flying	Navigator, Copilot	200 miles	Navigator's station; Copilot's control stand
9. Marker Beacon	RC-193A	Reception of location signals on navigation beams	Automatic	Local	Pilot's instrument panel
10. Long Range Navigation (Loran)	AN/APN-9 or AN/APN-9A	Indicates fixes for distance, location, and course	Navigator	750 miles daytime; 1200 miles night	Navigator's table
11. Radar	AN/APQ-13A (modified)	Radio detection and ranging	Radar Operator		Radar Operator's station
12. Doppler Drift	AN/APA-52	Auxiliary equipment for APQ-13A radar set	Radar Operator		Radar Operator's station
13. IFF	SCR-695	Automatic identification reply to challenge	Radar Operator	20 miles at 200 feet	Radar Operator's station
14. Instrument Approach	AN/ARN-5	Lateral and vertical glidepath indicator for approach to runway	Pilot	Local	Pilot's control stand
15. Radio Altimeter	SCR-718	Accurately measures vertical distance between ground and aircraft	Weather Observer	40,000 feet	Weather Observer's station
16. Weather Indicating	AN/AMQ-2	Measures outside temperature and relative humidity	Weather Observer		Weather Observer's station
17. Dinghy Transmitter	AN/CRT-3	Transmits distress signals in event aircraft is forced down	All crew members		Integral with unit
18. VHF Air-Sea Rescue	AN/CRC-7	Short range, two-way communication between grounded personnel and searching aircraft. Also transmits MCW signal.	All crew members	15 miles at 2000 feet	Integral with unit

TEST AIRCRAFT

In July 1951, three B-29s were modified as part of a full scale development program for airborne early warning. Both SAC and ADC were interested in the program. In this photograph is B-29-80-BW, 44-87599, equipped with an AN/APS-20C radar in the fairing on the forward fuselage. An additional fairing was installed under the aft fuselage beneath the national insignia. Blade ECM antennas also appear under the aft fuselage.   (USAF)

This ERB-29 had its tail number removed. Wing tip electronics pods were installed as was a QRC-1 antenna in the belly. A heavy lead weight was installed in the nose in order to retain center of gravity limits. This airplane was slated for delivery to the 55th SRW. This photograph, taken at Wright AFB, dates from early 1955.   (USAF)

Right: During the Korean Conflict, enemy night fighters took their toll on our bombers. As a counter to this threat, Project Glow Worm was instituted. This consisted of a 500,000,000 candlepower light coupled to the tail turret. The light would flash like a strobe in order to blind the enemy fighter pilot. Tests conducted in early 1953 at Wright AFB proved the light to be equally debilitating to the B-29 tail gunner and also made the airplane a better target for fighters not in line with the light.

(USAF Museum)

MONSTRO AND THE GOBLIN

One of the XF-85 Goblins approaches the trapeze.

Parasite fighters, to provide escort, had been around since the days of the dirigibles. With the advent of the 10,000-mile B-36, came the need for an adequate escort fighter, and tests were conducted with a pair of McDonnell XF-85 Goblin fighters and a B-29. The only airplane to carry the Goblin was EB-29B-60-BA, 44-48111. The aft bomb bay doors were removed, and a special trapeze mechanism was designed to fit into the bomb bay.

The XF-85 was 16 feet 3 inches in length, and had a 21 foot 1½ inch wingspan. Its wing area was a mere 90 square feet. The height was 8 feet 3¼ inches. With a 201-gallon fuel capacity, the Goblin grossed 4,550 pounds. While the airplane's handling characteristics were excellent, its recovery capabilities left much to be desired. Many of the recovery attempts resulted in landings on Muroc Lake.

The XF-85 was lowered into a pit and the B-29 was rolled over the fighter. The trapeze was extended in order to attach the Goblin, and then the trapeze and fighter were pulled into the aft bomb bay of the B-29.

XF-85, 46-523, with wing fins added, rests on its ground handling dolly. (Edwards AFB History Office)

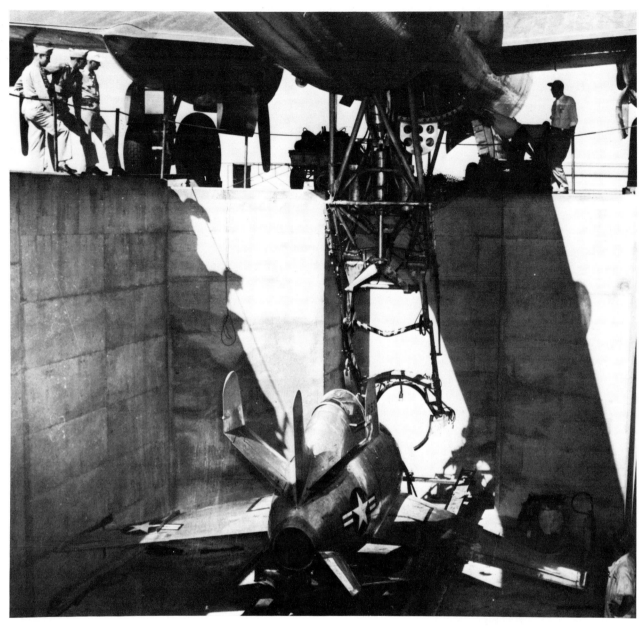

XF-85, 46-524, waits in the pit as the trapeze is lowered.

(Edwards AFB History Office)

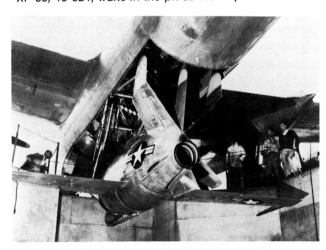

The fit of the Goblin in the aft bomb bay is checked.
(Edwards AFB History Office)

The Goblin is nestled in the aft bomb bay of Monstro.
(Edwards AFB History Office)

BELL X-1 CARRIER

The Bell X-1A, 48-1834, is shown launching from the mother B-29. (USAF)

In a joint program between the USAF, the National Advisory Committee for Aeronautics (NACA), and the Bell Aircraft Corporation, the X-1 series of research aircraft was built. The Bell X-1s carried serial numbers 46-062, 46-063, and 46-064. The first supersonic flight was made by Captain Charles E. "Chuck" Yeager on October 14, 1947. This was Yeager's 13th flight in the X-1, and the 50th for the X-1. Both the first and second aircraft combined to make up this total. Next came the Bell X-1A, X-1B, X-1C, X-1D, and X-1E series of aircraft. Each of these test aircraft was carried aloft in the belly of EB-29-96-BW, 45-21800. The bomb bay doors were removed and a special launch rack was installed in the bomb bay. A set of propellant dump tubes were mounted externally, aft of the bomb bay.

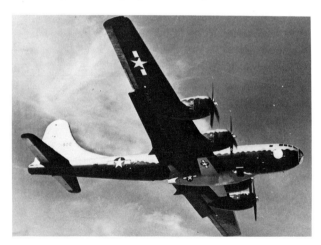

The second Bell XS-1, 46-063, was photographed on December 9, 1946, just prior to its first launch for powered flight. The pilot was Bell test pilot Chalmers "Slick" Goodlin. Note that the crew door was not installed on the XS-1 (later redesignated X-1). This photograph was taken just after takeoff - the B-29's nose gear had retracted, the main gear was coming up, and the flaps were extended. (USAF via Williams)

There was little ground clearance with the Bell X-1 tucked into the belly of the B-29 mother ship. (Edwards AFB History Office)

The EB-29 mother ship, replete with the Bell X-1B, 48-1385, visited Boeing Field in 1954.   (Olson via Williams)

In September 1955, the EB-29 and the X-1B were displayed at the Philadelphia Air Show. The NACA insignia had been applied to the tail, and the nose art was deleted.   (Williams)

Early in its career, the EB-29 had a black belly.
(Bowers)

Here the EB-29 is shown carrying the X-1A in 1955.
(Feist via Williams)

U.S. NAVY P2B

P2B-1, BuNo 84031, photographed at Van Nuys, California, in August 1949. Later this airplane would be redesignated as a P2B-2S. Scars from the former USAF tail number appear on the fin. All armament had been removed, and a radome had been installed in the forward lower turret location.

(Larkins)

A total of four B-29s were transferred to the U.S. Navy on April 14, 1947. These airplanes were redesignated as P2Bs and used as test beds for anti-submarine warfare programs and as mother ships for the Douglas D-558-2 Skyrocket. Two of the aircraft were equipped with bomb bay fuel tanks and test radar. These were redesignated as P2B-2Ss. A summary of the aircraft serial numbers follows:

BuNo	USN Designation	Block No.	USAF S/N	Remarks
84028	P2B-1S	B-29-95-BW	45-21789	
84029	P2B-1S	B-29-95-BW	45-21787	To NACA as 137
84030	P2B-2S	B-29-95-BW	45-21791	
84031	P2B-2S	B-29-90-BW	44-87766	

P2B-1S, BuNo 84029, prepares to launch the first all-rocket D-558-2 Skyrocket in the summer of 1951. This Skyrocket, ship No. 2, would be the first aircraft to exceed Mach 2 in level flight on November 20, 1953.

(via Museum of Flight)

BuNo 84029 was transferred to NACA for continuation of the supersonic flight test program. The Superfortress was redesignated as NACA-137. The mother ship had to be raised on jacks in order to load the Skyrocket. This same procedure was used to load the Bell X-1.

(via Museum of Flight)

TRAVIS AFB B-29

The airplane was subsequently converted into a TB-29 and then was transferred to the U.S. Navy for use as a target at the Naval Weapons Center at China Lake. Fortunately the airplane was spared destruction. This is the way the Travis Museum team found the airplane. She was dismantled and trucked to Travis for restoration. *(Korade)*

On December 22, 1944, B-29-25-MO, 42-65281, was delivered to the USAAF by the Glenn L. Martin Company, at Omaha, Nebraska. In January 1945, the airplane departed the United States under shipping code "Iron" through Hawaii. This airplane was assigned to the 6th Bombardment Group, 24th Bombardment Squadron. The unit was part of the 313th Bombardment Wing, stationed at North Field, Tinian.

All members of the original crew of 42-65281 were married. Several had children. The crew calculated that the earliest that one of their daughters could enter the Miss America Contest would be 1962; hence they named the airplane **Miss America '62.** Originally the airplane carried nose art on the right side of the airplane. The 6th BG identification of Triangle L was applied to the vertical tail, and several combat missions were flown with these markings. Then the edict came to "clean up their act," and the nose art was removed. The 6th BG pirate's head

insignia was applied to the nose, and the name was painted in the flame behind the pirate's head. Next the tail markings were changed to a Circle R. The plane-in-group number was 11.

In October 1945, 42-65281 returned to the United States and was reassigned to the 4196th Base Unit, Air Technical Services Command, at Robins Field, Georgia. The next assignment was the 301st BG, Strategic Air Command at Smoky Hill AFB, Kansas, between October 1948 and June 1949. The airplane was transferred to the Sacramento Air Materiel Area for conversion into the WB-29 configuration. In January 1951, the airplane was assigned to the 373rd Reconnaissance Squadron (Weather), MATS, at Kindley Air Base, Bermuda. In February of that year the unit was redesignated as the 53rd Strategic Reconnaissance Squadron (Weather). In October 1954, the airplane was reassigned to the Oklahoma Air Materiel Area. Next came a modification into the TB-29 configuration by the Crosley Division, Arso Manufacturing Corporation, at Berry Field, Nashville, Tennessee. The airplane was reassigned to the 3510th Combat Crew Training Wing, at Randolph AFB, Texas. The U.S. Navy obtained the airplane in November 1956, when it was transferred to China Lake, California.

The airplane now resides at Travis AFB, California, undergoing restoration for the base museum. It is being stripped of its former target tug markings and will be painted as she existed during World War II with the 6th BG.

*The second set of markings on **Miss America '62** were used when she served with the 24th Bomb Squadron, 6th Bomb Group, 313th Bomb Wing, based on Tinian. She carried the Circle R on the vertical tail and had the plane-in-group number 11 on the waist. She is seen here with 30 missions and two kills to her credit. Red, the 6th Bomb Group color, was applied to the fin tip.* *(Irvin)*

After serving with the 307th Bomb Group in Korea, B-29-25-MO, 42-65281, was stripped of its black belly color and converted into a WB-29. A "bug catcher" was installed at the aft upper turret location. The airplane was photographed while serving with the 53rd RS (M) Weather, flying out of Kindley Field, Bermuda. (USAF)

MODELER'S SECTION

Note: Since this book deals with derivatives of the B-29, no standard kits are available for review. Therefore, we are dispensing with our usual format for the "Modeler's Section," and are explaining the basics of how to begin the conversion for some of the derivatives covered. For the most part these conversions are rather difficult, and they are recommended only for the experienced modeler. In all cases, extensive research should be done on the specific aircraft being modeled.

KIT CONVERSIONS

F-13/RB-29

A photo-reconnaissance version of the B-29 may be constructed with varying degrees of difficulty. All of these airplanes had photo windows cut into the aft lower fuselage and a sight added forward of the nose gear doors. During World War II, all F-13s retained their armament. Post World War II RB-29s generally were unarmed and required deletion of all turrets and the filling of the resulting holes.

Yokohama Yo Yo, an F-13A, was built using the Airfix B-29 kit and decals from an IPMS sheet.   (Lloyd)

This Airfix 1/72nd scale kit was modified to a TB-29 target tug.   (Lloyd)

Tarzon Bomb Carrier

The forward lower turret must be replaced by an H2X radome similar to that carried on the SB-17 (available from 299 Models of Seattle, Washington). The bomb bay doors and bomb bay center section must be trimmed to fit a scratch-built Tarzon bomb.

Mother Ships

A number of mother ship versions of the B-29 may be built to carry a variety of babies. In all cases, the armament must be deleted. The bomb bays must be modified according to the baby carried. The following supplemental kits are available in 1/72 scale:

XF-85 Goblin	- Airmodel
Bell X-1	- Airvac
Bell X-1A/X-1E	- Airvac
Douglas D-558 Skyrocket	- KR Models

So Tired, Seven-to-Seven is an RB-29A made from the Airfix kit and Microscale decals.   (Lloyd)

WB-29

With the exception of the few armed B-29s employed by AWS during the Korean Conflict, all armament should be deleted from a model of a WB-29. Depending upon the version, appropriate psychrometers, antennas, and "bug catchers" must be added.

This B-29 was assigned to the 308th Reconnaissance Group (Weather). The markings on the model were the result of careful painting and the use of a variety of decals. *(Lloyd)*

This WB-29, assigned to the 59th Reconnaissance Squadron (Weather), was named **Polar Queen.** In addition to the black belly, she carried arctic red paint on the empennage and outer wing panels. Antennas and psychrometers were added to the model. *(Lloyd)*

KB-29 TANKERS

Both the KB-29M hose and drogue tanker and KB-29P boom tanker may be built as a conversion from the basic bomber. In all cases, the armament must be deleted. For the hose and drogue tanker, a refueling drogue must be added to the aft lower fuselage. In the case of the KB-29P, a set of refueling director lights must be added to the bomb bay door, a stiffener must be added to each side of the aft lower fuselage, and a refueling boom and boom support must be added.

This KB-29M, from the 421st ARefS, has a hose and drogue system built into the aft lower fuselage. *(Lloyd)*

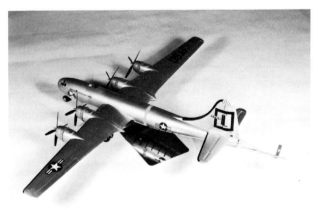

A refueling boom from a RAREplanes KC-97 and a scratchbuilt boom support were added to make this KB-29P from the 91st ARefS. A spare waist blister was added to the former tail gun position to serve as an observation port for the boom operator. *(Lloyd)*

A-Bombers

Construction of the atomic bombers is relatively straight forward. All armament must be deleted except for the tail guns. The holes for the fuselage turrets must be plugged.

The three blisters on the aft fuselage must be deleted. The plugs for the waist blisters had relatively small rectangular windows. In 1/48th scale, the Monogram kit includes both a Fat Man and a Little Boy bomb.

*The Monogram 1/48th scale B-29 was used to build this model of **Bockscar**.* (Monogram)

DECALS

Detail & Scale Volume 10, B-29 Superfortress, Production Versions, carried a complete list of available decals in both 1/72 and 1/48 scales designed specifically for the B-29. In addition, several other sheets contain decals which may be used for bits and pieces. These include:

- Microscale Sheet No. 72-187 contains SAC insignia and a "Milky Way" band.
- Microscale Sheet No. 72-190 contains MATS, rescue, and weather lettering.
- Microscale Sheets No. 72-458 and 48-236 carry Air Rescue markings.
- Microscale Sheets No. 72-195 and 72-242 carry American flags and Navy markings.
- Microscale Sheets No. 72-132 and 48-133 have USAF lettering.
- Microscale Sheets No. 72-188 and 48-132 have U.S. AIR FORCE lettering.
- Microscale Sheet No. 48-288 has U.S. national insignia.
- Scale-Master Sheet SM-18 contains U.S. AIR FORCE lettering.
- Scale-Master Sheet SM-28 contains 15th AF insignia.
- Scale-Master Sheet SM-31 contains 8th AF insignia.